ONCE UPON a RHYME

POEMS FROM THE UK

Edited by Donna Samworth

First published in Great Britain in 2011 by:

 Young**Writers**

Young Writers
Remus House
Coltsfoot Drive
Peterborough
PE2 9BF
Telephone: 01733 890066
Website: www.youngwriters.co.uk

THIS BOOK BELONGS TO

....

FOREWORD

Here at Young Writers our objective is to help children discover the joys of poetry and creative writing. Few things are more encouraging for the aspiring writer than seeing their own work in print. We are proud that our anthologies are able to give young authors this unique sense of confidence and pride in their abilities.

Once Upon A Rhyme is our latest fantastic competition, specifically designed to encourage the writing skills of primary school children through the medium of poetry. From the high quality of entries received, it is clear that Once Upon A Rhyme really captured the imagination of all involved.

The resulting collection is an excellent showcase for the poetic talents of the younger generation and we are sure you will be charmed and inspired by it, both now and in the future.

Contents

MADDIE STEWART IS OUR FEATURED POET THIS YEAR. SHE HAS WRITTEN A NONSENSE WORKSHOP FOR YOU AND INCLUDED SOME OF HER GREAT POEMS. YOU CAN FIND THESE IN THE MIDDLE OF YOUR BOOK.

Sibertswold CE Primary School, Shepherdswell

Thirsk CP School, Thirsk

Vaughan Primary School, West Harrow

Victoria Primary School, Carrickfergus

Warren Hills CP School, Coalville

Ysgol Hiraddug, Dyserth

THE POEMS

I Want To Be . . . A-Z

I want to be an armadillo,
I want to be a bee,
I want to be a crocodile
Swimming in the sea.

I want to be a dinosaur,
I want to be an elephant,
I want to be a frog,
As green as can be.

I want to be a goat,
I want to be a hippo,
I want to be an iguana,
Strolling through the grass.

I want to be a jaguar,
I want to be a kangaroo,
I want to be a lion,
That roars and shouts, *'Boohoo!'*

I want to be a monkey,
I want to be a narwhale,
I want to be an ostrich
And I want to be a pig.

I want to be a quail,
I want to be a rhino,
I want to be a snake
And I want to be a T-rex.

I want to be a uakari,
I want to be a vulture,
I want to be a walrus
And an X-ray fish!

I also want to be a yak
And a zebra mouse, hey!

Holly-Louise Davies (11)

1

Sky Invaders

As they come closer and closer
To destroy the world, I read
They will destroy us all to just breed,
What greed.

I see them, see them coming,
Coming for us, what will the army do?
What can they do?
All that can happen is getting eaten like salami.

We will all die in an undelightful way,
They don't understand us so we cannot say,
What a shame on a wonderful day.

The aliens are coming,
Coming to change the Earth,
And this is just for one reason,
Only to give birth.

They can see me,
Looking very hungry, they will eat me,
Eat me very hard, this won't be merry,
I will die hard.

How, how will they win?
They will win so good
But for once I will be
Hiding behind a tin can.

Jordan Heylligar (10)

Animal Kingdom

Animals, animals, lots around
Some lie in water and some on the ground
They have their own special language to talk to each other
The little babies call to their mother

With tigers and lions stalking their prey
And gorillas and chimps having fun every day
Mice so small
And huge elephants so tall
Animals, there are lots to see

Huge eagles so strong
And big pythons so long
Big rhinos, grey with very hard skin
Try racing a cheetah, you won't ever win
Animals, there are lots to see

Fluffy dogs barking all the time
Cuddly cats with green eyes that shine
Big black bats flapping around
Horses neighing, that's their sound

Come to the world of animals.

Amelia Harris Hall (10)

Cats

Cuddly little animals
Big and small
No matter what size
Just watch as time goes by
Then start to make a picture.

Lois Cook (10)

A Poem To Be Spoken Silently
(Inspired by 'A Poem to be Spoken Silently' by Pie Corbett)

It was so quiet I could hear
the wind slowly drifting away
back to its dark cloud.

It was so silent I could hear
a mouse happily squeaking
because it found lots of cheese.

It was so quiet I could hear
baby birds cheeping for food
miles away in the distance.

It was so quiet I could hear
little baby insects squeaking under the pavement
trying to get out and find their mum.

It was so quiet I could hear
an aeroplane zoom in the sky at top speed
while cutting through the terrified clouds.

Datela Kubelabo (10)

Sadness

Sadness, guilt, despair,
The colour of darkness, there's no light.
There's no day,
Only dark and night.
Walking through a graveyard
With dark spirits all around you
Walking through your body,
It feels like they're walking
Through your grave.
You shiver and shiver,
Oh you feel so alone.

Destiny Grant (8)

All The Time

All the time
They just play with others
And they leave people out
They just cry and cry
And pretend they don't notice me.

All the time
But they always stare at me
As if they want to fight
I am really terrified
And I wonder what might happen.

All the time
I can feel it in my heart
That they want to hurt me
I try to move away
But they come in my nightmares.

Hanaa Bennis (8)

Terror Murders

The terror, the horror, oh my
It's approaching
Ever so quicker than the speed of sound.
Here we go again
Another crime scene on the way.
Look at the CCTV
There must be some footage.
Any fingerprints?
No, not yet.
Try to find who murdered the Queen.

Adam Ghafor (9)

The Sparkling Sea

The sparkling sea
As big as 100,000,000 buildings
Vast, gigantic, immense
Like a massive country stretching round the world
It makes me feel like a bug
The sparkling sea
How I wish I could see it all.

Joseph Crouthers Camacho (10)

The High Street

Lots of people visit
Huge, immense and busy
As long as the sky itself
More noisy than a monkey on a lawnmower
The best thing in life
Insignificant as a dot on paper
The high street
What's with the fashions?

Joshua Williams (10)

Silence

Silence is the colour of grey clouds floating in the sky
Silence smells like the air all around us
Silence sounds like the fresh green grass
Silence tastes like thin air up above
Silence looks like a picture hanging on the wall
Silence feels like a feeling to me
Silence reminds me of Mrs Clark
When she is in the classroom on her own.

Elle Louise Hodgkinson (8)

Princess

One day there was a princess.
She was playing
In the garden.
One day
She heard a noise.
She ran to it,
She saw two chicks.
One was yellow
And one was black.
They were fluffy.
She took them inside.
She played with them
Until they grew up.
She let them go.
The princess missed her chicks
And they missed her,
But they never returned.
The princess was very sad.

Adilah Peerbaccus (8)
Beehive Prep School, Ilford

The Magical Island

There is a magical island
And a magical castle,
There are lots of magical mushrooms
And a big monster guarding it.
The monster is coloured purple.
The land sleeps,
The night falls,
And the prince saves the princess.
What a beautiful fairy tale,
And a happy ending.

Zayd Ahmed (7)
Beehive Prep School, Ilford

Magical Animals

Into the enchanted forest
I journeyed
In the search for magical animals.
It was not dark
In the forest.
The grass was as orange
As an orange,
The water in the stream
Was absolutely clear.
I jumped over it
And met a brown horse.
It had wings
The size of a small aeroplane.
When it saw me
It jumped and flew into the air.
It was much faster
Than any aeroplane I had seen
And in a second
It had cleared the forest.
I saw a cat
That could breathe underwater
And a bee which spoke in English,
'Can't stop, buzz, buzz,' it said,
'Lots of honey to make.'
I walked happily home,
Pleased with my result
And that was how
I found out about magical animals.

Himanshu Singh (8)
Beehive Prep School, Ilford

The Carpet In The Living Room

I have a carpet in the living room,
It takes me everywhere.
I went to a magic ocean,
All glittery and shiny,
There was a mermaid,
All pretty and nice,
She needed help.
All dangerous and exciting it was,
When it was 7am
I told my carpet to go home.
I tried to sneak in,
My mum said, 'Where have you been?'
I said, 'To my friend's house.'
Shhh, it's our secret,
My mum will never know!

Madiha Liaquat (8)
Beehive Prep School, Ilford

Underground

Underground
I think I heard something.
Underground.
I went inside
To tell Mom.
She said, 'Don't be silly!'
So I went to my dad,
He said, 'Stop being silly.'
Then I went outside
And got my shovel
And I dug and dug.
I saw . . .
Well, what did I see?
No one will ever know!

Dillon Gunputh (8)
Beehive Prep School, Ilford

Life In Space

Space is the place
That doesn't have any air.
Space is the place
That has nine planets
And we have no clues
If there are any aliens.
The biggest bit is the sun,
With sunspots and flares.
There is a Milky Way,
The galaxy,
And I will never forget
The black hole
That takes you to a new universe.
We never know if you will survive.
There's the moon
And flare lights.
Oh yes,
There's such a big life
In space
And you'll never guess what I've found -
An alien!

Adem Gezgin (8)
Beehive Prep School, Ilford

Magic Pumpkin

Magic pumpkin,
Magic pumpkin,
Where can you be?
I think you're up a tree, no,
Or maybe down in a burrow, no.
Are you up or down,
Or left or right?
Tell me, Pumpkin,
Tell me, Pumpkin,
Where are you?
Oh, magic pumpkin,
Magic pumpkin,
Where can you be?

Anjali Tohani (8)
Beehive Prep School, Ilford

The Castle

It was a nice sunny day.
You could see magical mushrooms,
Magical trees,
Magical floor
And magical air.
A knight goes into the castle.
He defeats all the creatures
Then the knight faces a 20 foot tall bat
And the castle blows fire.
The knight gets some fire
With his sword.
He burns the bat,
He saves the princess,
They run out of the castle
Because it was destroyed.

Kas Barlas (8)
Beehive Prep School, Ilford

The Beautiful Sea

The sea is so beautiful,
It's better than peas.
Rocking up and down,
The waves of the beautiful sea.
Boats sailing across,
Pirates say, 'Ahoy!'
Because there's nothing better
Than the sea.
Waves washing, pirates saying, 'Ahoy!'
Speedboats rushing past you,
Sailors fishing from a cliff,
That's what's best about the sea.
Dolphins jumping up,
Also fishes too,
Sharks creeping under you,
People swimming in the waves.
It is so beautiful,
Why don't you try it for yourselves?

Abu Arifeen Khan (9)
Beehive Prep School, Ilford

The Magical Land

One morning
I woke up very funny.
The sun was purple and glittery,
Animals were flying
High in the sky.
The sky was red,
The trees were blue.
There's nothing
In a magical land to do.
The grass was yellow,
Yellow as sand.
I ran outside,
I was living in a big castle.
I played in the grass,
I ran in the grass.
There's nothing like a
Magical land.

Sumaiya Ghafoor (8)
Beehive Prep School, Ilford

The Princess

The princess was stuck in a castle.
A dragon guarded the castle.
Every day she would look outside the window
And say, 'Why won't somebody rescue me?'
One day she saw a knight
And waved at him.
He ran up to the princess.
The princess saw the dragon
And said, 'You didn't kill the dragon!'
They just got away.
They got to his castle
But the knight was so lazy
The princess said,
'I was better off in that castle.'

Nafeesa Aziz (9)
Beehive Prep School, Ilford

The Magical Animals

I know a place,
There are magical animals.
We laugh and play together
Every single day.
But one night
They were gone.
Their names are
Doney and Johnny.
I went on a search
To find them,
I checked in their homes
And there they were,
Just looking after their mum's babies.

Usama Uddin (8)
Beehive Prep School, Ilford

Down Into The Underground

Down, down,
Into the underground.
Hey, look what I found.
I found a hundred pounds
And a precious crown.
Up, up, up I go.
I found myself
To watch a show.
But then I thought
The queue was too slow,
So I went out
To watch the Thames river flow.

Rea Robinson (8)
Beehive Prep School, Ilford

13

The Gold Castle

I went to the gold castle,
Surrounded by trees and bushes.
I saw some gold
In the gold castle.
I saw a few people
Rushing, they were carrying gold
In the gold castle.
There was a magic river outside
With skyscrapers beside it
Next to the gold castle.
It was a magical place
In the gold castle.

Iram Ahmed (8)
Beehive Prep School, Ilford

The Magic Road

I found a magic road
I followed the magic road
I arrived at a castle
I saw a dragon
I fought the dragon
I climbed to the highest room in the castle
I came to the room
I looked behind the curtain
I saw a princess and saved her
The princess and I got married
And lived happily ever after.

Rai Singh Bansal (7)
Beehive Prep School, Ilford

Victoria, Queen Of England

V ictoria lost her uncle when she was only eighteen
I n 1837 she became queen
C hristened Alexandrina Victoria, she was
    the daughter of Prince Edward
T he queen got married at the age of twenty-one,
    to her cousin Albert
O pera, singing and painting were some of her favourite pastimes
R evolution saw England become the most powerful
    and richest country
I ndustries grew, mining, manufacturing and transport
    were all developed
A lbert died in 1861 at the age of forty-two and Victoria,
    in her grief, wore black for the rest of her reign.

Cassidy Bell (10)
Cherry Dale Primary School, Cudworth

Sports

I really do love sports and games,
All the big players, all the big names.
Some need a bat, some need a ball,
Whatever the sport, I love them all!

Some players are good, some are bad,
Just win the game, don't make me sad.
My favourite sport is football, how about you?
And my favourite team is Man U!

Kane Joburns (10)
Cherry Dale Primary School, Cudworth

Football Crazy

Who loves football? I love football.
Strike the ball, what a goal!
A goal up already, I like football,
Everyone likes football.
Dive for the ball, what a save!
Fantastic game, well done team.
Another game well played.

Cameron Keenan (10)
Cherry Dale Primary School, Cudworth

My Rabbit

My rabbit is called Belle,
She doesn't really smell!
She is black and white
And doesn't like to fight.
She doesn't bite,
She doesn't nip,
But I really do love her to bits.

Elle-Mae Hopkins (10)
Cherry Dale Primary School, Cudworth

Strawberry Shortcake

The way I awake
Like a strawberry shortcake,
The candles I display
All over my face,
Light up my life,
Like the best birthday cake!

Olivia Miles (10)
Cherry Dale Primary School, Cudworth

The Crazy And Lazy Harvest

The wheat is so sweet
And it is a treat
When the mango tangos
With the cherries
But not the berries
This made the pear
Very unfair
There was a barn
On the farm
The evil lime
Did a very bad crime
All the fruit
Played the flute.
Harvest - what a busy time!

Joshua Gardner (11)
Chiddingly Primary School, Lewes

Harvest Is Coming

Harvest is ready,
Sparrows eat marrows,
The wheat has a beat,
Cherries and berries are
Ripe and ready,
Harvest is ready.

Harvest is ready,
Rice is diced,
Mangos do tangos
On the cooling ice,
Harvest is ready.

Harvest is ready,
I dance with mice
Till the light has
Faded like rice,
Harvest is ready.

Harvest is now,
The cow goes moo,
Birds like delicate
Fairies coo,
Harvest is now.

Isabel Wright (11)
Chiddingly Primary School, Lewes

The Wheat Is So Sweet

The wheat is so sweet, a delight, it is a treat,
But the cauliflower came out sour,
And the rice was so nice that it got eaten by mice,
I saw a bat with a hat and is all this a fact?

Kara-Rose Francis (9)
Chiddingly Primary School, Lewes

Groove

Wheat has a beat
My wheat grew and got reckless
And went to the street.

Walking along it met some corn
And the corn stepped on a thorn
On its way to the lawn.

The cabbage rolled over
And got torn.

The wheat found a field
And then reeled
Everyone in.

And then the farmer
Threw us in the bin.

Rowan Nichols (10)
Chiddingly Primary School, Lewes

Harvest Party

As the mangos
Do their famous tangos,
The juicy tomato
Does the staccato,
With a marrow
Wielding a barrow.

The wheat
Is so sweet,
While the lemon's power
Is amazingly sour,
The corn's in the silo,
But the cow's called Milo.

There are combines
In many lines,
There's a farmer
That rides a llama,
And the llama's a pig,
It eats a whole fig
And then goes for a jig!

Daisy Fierek (11)
Chiddingly Primary School, Lewes

Harvest

It's harvest time
With lemon and lime,
The mice in the barn
Are looking for yarn
To get snug for winter,
Without getting a splinter.

The fruit is a loot
With the wheat
And the beet,
While the corn
With the thorns
Is very forlorn.

The wheat in the field
Is using a shield
To stop the combine
Cutting its long line.
It's harvest time
With lemon and lime.

Emma Carter (10)
Chiddingly Primary School, Lewes

Harvest Is Here

The wheat is so sweet
As it tickles my feet,
I danced with the pig
As I stamped on a fig,
The pig ate a mango
As he played the banjo,
I tackled the apple
As the fruit played the flute,
Harvest is so nice,
Just like the rice,
So smile for a while
Because harvest is here.

Megan Bridger (10)
Chiddingly Primary School, Lewes

Such A Sight I Saw

As the birds fly by
Soaring through the sky
The wheat is so sweet
A delight, it's a treat
So let's sit back and relax
Sipping white wine
Watching the berries grow in a line
The rice was so nice
That it got eaten by mice
But the tender cauliflower
Turned out sour.

Daisy-May Anscombe (9)
Chiddingly Primary School, Lewes

Dance Did The Berries

When I went to get the cherries,
Dance did the berries,
While the mango did a tango
And my friend played the banjo.

So fed up with that,
I went to get the cat
Who was chasing the mice,
Who were after the rice.

Down goes the cat,
And that is that!

Gemma Longley (9)
Chiddingly Primary School, Lewes

Musical Harvest

As I entered a room,
Which was a silly thing to do,
I saw some fruit playing the flute
And playing with that was an avocado
Playing the piano!
And as I looked round the corner
I saw a great palaver, as a mango
Started to do the tango!
And at the end of the room
I saw a pig playing the banjo with a broom.

Rosie Fieldwick (9)
Chiddingly Primary School, Lewes

The Wheat

The wheat is so sweet,
In my little feet,
I felt the cherries
And the little berries,
Hanging off the tree,
Then a thought came to me,
I knew I was turning into an apple tree,
At least I can pick apples off me, the tree!

Lewis Jones (9)
Chiddingly Primary School, Lewes

The Wheat Is So Sweet

The wheat is so sweet,
I collected cherries and berries,
I tangoed with the mango,
The cauliflower came out sour,
The mice ate the rice
Harvest is as cool as ice.

Harrison Commons (9)
Chiddingly Primary School, Lewes

Harvest Delight

The cherries seemed to dance with the berries,
The mangos did a tango,
The wheat went all sweet,
Veg went over the hedge,
The mice ate all the nice rice,
Someone sliced the dice.

Ella Tenoski-Fenn (9)
Chiddingly Primary School, Lewes

I Tangoed With A Mango

I tangoed with a mango
When in the moonlight and the gloom,
I ate a juicy fig whilst I danced with a pig,
The rice was so nice,
The swede hit the weed,
The parrots ate the carrots,
And the moon went home,
The sun came out,
That's what harvest is all about.

Millie Harris (10)
Chiddingly Primary School, Lewes

PS3

I like my car game,
It is hard like rock.
I'm loving it.
It is shaped like a box.
It is my favourite thing,
It helps me have fun.
I can play the game.
It is black like a blackboard.
It is a wireless computer.

Kyle Phillips (10)
Danygraig Primary School, Port Tennant

Love

Roses are red
Violets are blue
You are cute
And that is true

Roses are red
Violets are blue
Tesco.com will deliver
To you

Roses are red
Violets are blue
I love to sing
But only with you

Roses are red
Violets are blue
You are cool
But not a fool

Roses are red
Violets are blue
Love never crossed my mind
Until I met you.

Bailey Garner (10)
Danygraig Primary School, Port Tennant

My Dog

My dog plays all day
My dog runs round in the garden all the time
My dog loves going for walks
My dog always drinks his water
My dog likes getting belly rubs
My dog is full of all different covers over his body
My dog will never back down from a fight
My dog loves busting balls and playing in goals.

Jay Niewiadomski (10)
Danygraig Primary School, Port Tennant

Best Friends

My best friend Gemma,
She is the bestest friend ever,
We play in the park,
Light and dark,
We eat ice cream,
Sit down and talk by the stream,
We love to dance,
We're taking a chance,
We love art,
We'll never be apart,
We love sleepovers,
We ride in our mum's Rover,
We make each other laugh,
Even when we're in the bath,
We learn to trust,
Oh yes, we must,
We're animal lovers,
We play with each other's,
We care for each other,
Look after one another,
We are best friends.

Carla Harris (10)
Danygraig Primary School, Port Tennant

My Rabbit

My rabbits have bobby tails,
They play with a whale,
They like chomping on their lettuce,
Jumping in the muddy puddles,
The only problem is they poo everywhere.
They have loads of bumps
And they thump on the floor.
They have cute, fluffy bodies.
Best of all, they love me and they care.

Tammy Drewson Alli (10)
Danygraig Primary School, Port Tennant

My Best Friend

My best friend is funny
My best friend is cool
She has a thing for school
She is a star of acting
She helps a lot of the time
She loves apples and cherries
But she hates sprouts
She loves horses
She loves horse riding
She has two fish that are purple
She has a brother called Adam Thomas
She is ten years old
She helps me when I'm sad
My best friend is friendly
My best friend is Sophie.

Rhiannon Davies (10)
Danygraig Primary School, Port Tennant

My Best Friend

My best friend is funny
My best friend is cool
She walks with me to school
She thinks the world of me
But she has been stung by a bee
We have so much fun
Playing in the hot sun
She and I love apples and cherries
We eat so much we have bad bellies
We make each other laugh and dance
While wearing red underpants
She has a dog called Roxy
And her favourite character is Foxy Loxy
My best friend is Rhiannon.

Sophie Lynnette Thomas (11)
Danygraig Primary School, Port Tennant

My Best Friend

My best friend is funny
My best friend is cool
She walks with me to school
She thinks the world of me
We have so much fun playing in the sun
We hear birds tweeting, then we hear girls weeping
She and I love apples and cherries
We eat so much
We have bad bellies
We make each other laugh and dance
While wearing red underpants
She has three dogs called Fiss, Jess and Stella
That's my best friend Tara-Lee.

Chloe Vodden (10)
Danygraig Primary School, Port Tennant

Barclays Premier League

Transfers done, they are fun
Goals galore, score more than four
Rumours and new Puma togs
'Match of the Day', too much pay
Fans and Man of the Match
Stadiums and fading sounds
Loud sounds and rounds, grounds
Home and away, Liverpool stay away
Skills and spills all over the pitch
Goals and fans
Raw skills and fouls
That is the Barclays Premier League.

Jack Dicataldo (10)
Danygraig Primary School, Port Tennant

Cars

Cars are cool
Cars are rusty
Cars are fast
And cars are slow
And I like cars when
Their engine roars
And that is why I like my cars.

Cameron Davies (10)
Danygraig Primary School, Port Tennant

My Dog

My dog rants and raves, he digs a grave
My dog has spots and little dots
My dog is so cute, he bites my flute
My dog loves to play all day
My dog loves the park until it's dark
My dog is as small as a ball.

Adam Duffy (10)
Danygraig Primary School, Port Tennant

The Black Jaguar

The black jaguar comes at night
As people are frightened of his bite.
He prowls around without making a sound
As the last thing he wants is to be found.
The big black jaguar isn't all he seems,
He's just a big cat that purrs and gleams.

James Davies (10)
Danygraig Primary School, Port Tennant

Fun

Fun is yellow,
Everyone's friend.
Fun is green,
Sprinting on the grass.
Fun is red,
You're smiling with laughter.
Fun is blue,
Looking up into the sky.
Fun is pink,
Loving every moment.
Fun is white,
You're laying on clouds.
Fun is turquoise,
Swimming in the sea.
Fun is fantastic,
Everyone's friend!

Lucy Robbens (11)
Foxborough Middle School, Lowestoft

Summer Is . . .

Summer is the sun in the morning when the birds sing.
Summer is the children playing in the sand.
Summer is the regatta raft race in the freezing cold sea.
Summer is the adults coping with children in the sea.
Summer is the teenagers sunbathing on the sand.
Summer is party time.
Summer is the climbing frame.
Summer is the field in the afternoon.
Summer is fun.

Millie Whittall (9)
Gerrans School, Truro

Snowy Winter

At the start of winter
The brown, hungry squirrels collect their nuts
Ready for the weather coming their way.
Wet washing showers pour on the roofs of houses,
Flaming fires bursting through chimneys.

In the middle of winter
The snow starts to pour white, wicked drops of rain,
No grass in sight, just cold, fuzzy white,
No more school, holidays are here,
Summer is far, but Christmas is near.

At the end of winter
Presents at the ready.
Christmas Eve tonight, so warm and snuggly,
All the Christmas specials are on the TV,
On the sofa with the fire crackling.

On Christmas Day we wake up early,
Sneak downstairs and get a Curly-Wurly,
Wake Mum, see all the presents,
Open them up, see all the surprises.
Next up, roast dinner, turkey on the dock,
Carrots, potatoes, stuffing and gravy, yum-yum.

Christmas is over and so is winter.
Spring is here once again.
Say goodbye to Christmas until next year.

Lauryn Mitchell (10)
Gerrans School, Truro

29

Sizzling Summer

The sizzling summer has come once again
And everyone's as cheerful as ever,
The sea feels warm but cool as well
And we swam till our hearts were content.
The sun popped up and was dancing like a girl on stage,
While we were playing volleyball on the beach.
We were building sandcastles until
They were as high as the sky.
Finally we walked up the hill,
Back to my house
And said goodbye to the sizzling summer.

Georgina Savage (10)
Gerrans School, Truro

Summer Versus Winter

One summer day
Blazing hot weather
Growing trees branch over branch
Rabbits hopping like fleas on a dog
Trips to never before
Insects buzzing flower to flower

Snow as white as clouds
Helping my rabbit keep warm
Scooping snow to make snow cream
Forests of ice as iron
Enemies battling with snow
Snowflakes like stars drifting down to the ground
Snow angels like gods on the ground.

Ben Clarke (10)
Gerrans School, Truro

Summer Poem

Summer is like going to bed.
In summer you can go for picnics on the sands.
In summer you can play at the seaside.
In summer, when it's the holidays, you can stay up late.
Summer is like playing on the beach and
Eating ice creams on the coast.
When it's dark outside in the summer, you can watch movies.
Summer is as hot as the sun.
Summer is like going cycling in hot sunshine.
Summer is like playing on the beach with Callum.
Summer is like having the hot sun on your skin, burning away.
Summer is like seeing heat waves every day on the ground.

Conway Gilbert (8)
Gerrans School, Truro

Dazzling December

Deer are resting in the starless night
When the moon is shining upon them.
Children are dozing by listening
To the sweet sound chimes
Swaying in the breeze.
Streets are pitch-black, with lights
Reflecting on the deep, white snow.
Santa is getting his strong brown reindeer
Ready for the biggest night of their lives,
Which means Christmas is finally here.

Victoria Chaffin (10)
Gerrans School, Truro

Winter

Winter is bread and warm cookies in the bakery.
Winter is bells chiming.
Winter is smoke coming out of people's chimneys.
Winter is Santa coming to my house.
Winter is boys having snowball fights.

Oliver Shaw (8)
Gerrans School, Truro

Mixed Summer And Winter

Winter is a snowball fight.
The snow is as white as a cloud.
I build a snowman.
I love energy because it's fun in the snow.

I like summer.
I like ice creams, they are tasty.
I like the beach because
I can swim and play and sunbathe.

Olivia Grahamslaw (7)
Gerrans School, Truro

Winter's Rushing

Winter is cold like frozen ice.
Winter is trees rustling in the wind.
Winter is snow falling gently.
Winter is lightning thrashing against steel.
Winter is thunder crashing up the streets.

Ned Collins (7)
Gerrans School, Truro

Summertime

Summer is like sun burning on your skin.
Summer is time for ice cream on the beach.
Summer is building sandcastles at the seaside.
Summer is the start of the cricket season.
Summer is my birthday.
Summer is staying at Portsmouth.

Joseph Tilley (8)
Gerrans School, Truro

Summery Spring

In summery spring all the flowers *spring* to life
Just like they have been dead for winter.
All the trees have exploded
With leaves all sorts of greens.
All the fluffy lambs are
Bouncing about like an excited child.
The trees are no longer bare as a button.
The vegetables are growing
For the horticultural show.
And that is summery spring.

Saphia Williams (10)
Gerrans School, Truro

Emotions Of Autumn

Autumn's first sunrise is like the first flame on a bonfire.
In autumn, trees can be as blank as a piece of paper.
Thunder howls like a wolf on a full moon.
Sometimes leaves can fall so fast like a sports car in a race.
Flowers hide from the raging rain and wind.
Crushing leaves are like the first strike of lightning.
The gloomy first day of autumn is at an end.
The fireworks were like shooting stars racing in the sky.

Truran Chaffin (10)
Gerrans School, Truro

The Winter Poem

The winter snow is sparkling.
The winter is for making big snowmen.
The winter is for tasting the snow.
The snow freezes into ice.
The ice makes the cars slip.

Samantha Mitchell (8)
Gerrans School, Truro

If I Was A Meerkat

(Inspired by 'If I Had Wings' by Pie Corbett)

If I was a meerkat,
I would listen to all danger
And would stand like a statue.

If I was a meerkat,
I would nibble at nuts
For the winter.

If I was a meerkat,
I would scent all the air
As the meerkats stood still.

If I was a meerkat,
I would gaze for miles and miles.

If I was a meerkat,
I would pat on the sand
As I built my burrow.

If I was a meerkat,
I would listen to all the
Meerkats' gossip.

If I was a meerkat,
I would like all the sweetness
Of our nuts.

If I was a meerkat,
I would whiff the long, dry grass
As I hid.

If I was a meerkat,
I would peer through the bushes
As hunters spy.

If I was a meerkat,
I would pat the mud silently
In the daylight.

Alice Hefford (9)
Hartwell CE Primary School, Hartwell

If I Had Super Powers
(Inspired by 'If I Had Wings' by Pie Corbett)

If I had super powers,
I would fly as high as a bird and gaze at the buildings
As I soared through the air.

If I had super powers,
I would hear the wind whistle in my ears
As I went super-speed.

If I had super powers,
I would be as fast as a cheetah.

If I had super powers,
I would smash through the walls and
Crash down on villains like an avalanche.

If I had super powers,
I would squeeze two cars together
Like two lumps of cheese.

If I had super powers,
I would be as strong as an elephant.

If I had super powers,
I would be as invisible as the air in the sky.

If I had super powers,
I would taste danger as I walked,
When I was invisible.

If I had super powers,
I would scent the villainous evil
When the world was in need of help.

If I had super powers,
I would save the world from evil villains
Around the planet.

Matthew Webster (9)
Hartwell CE Primary School, Hartwell

If I Were A Dog
(Inspired by 'If I Had Wings' by Pie Corbett)

If I were a dog,
I would see a transparent cloud
Drift slowly across the deserted world
And lick the fresh water from the stream,
Delicate and beautiful.

If I were a dog,
I would sniff the sweet flowers
Of the meadow in the valley
And pad softly over the lush green grass
As soft as velvet.

If I were a dog,
I would feel the soft, silky hearth rug
Next to the roaring village of fire
And turn over on my back
To feel it once more.

If I were a dog,
I would taste the spring air
Refreshing my mind into
A clear, fresh mist,
Lasting forever and ever.

If I were a dog,
I would hear a sudden loud bark
Echoing in my head
And the magical birds bursting into song.

If I were a dog,
I would remember all of my
Treasured memories and happiness
I had in my early days.

Emily Heron (9)
Hartwell CE Primary School, Hartwell

If I Had My Own Planet
(Inspired by 'If I Had Wings' by Pie Corbett)

If I had my own planet,
I would feel the magic rocks
At the bottom of the ocean,
That make you live forever.

If I had my own planet,
I would watch torchlights
From magic, airborne people.

If I had my own planet,
I would listen to constant music
Playing in my head.

If I had my own planet,
I would gobble special food
To keep me young.

If I had my own planet,
I would sniff the iffy pong
Washing out in the air.

If I had my own planet,
I would call it Varserthetro
And make people with big eyes.

If I had my own planet,
I would be the most
Powerful man in the world.

John Reed (9)
Hartwell CE Primary School, Hartwell

The Wave

The wave looks like a relentless cobra
Vigorously stretching out at its vulnerable prey.
The turbulent wave lustily grew,
Until it finally leapt at the surfer.
The audacious surfer was microscopic
Compared to the humongous wave.

Elliott Anderson (10)
Hartwell CE Primary School, Hartwell

The Wave

The growing wave towers over me
Like a humungous, clawed hand
Reaching surreptitiously for its meek prey.
A low growling sound; a pugnacious bull
Snorting at its courageous challenger.
The soft blue creeps beneath me
Whilst I anxiously crouch,
Not taking my eyes off the bleary horizon.
But it grows,
It grows like microscopic plankton
Growing into a grumbling piranha.
The water scintillates as I surf down,
Down, down, down.
The moist spray flicks its blood towards me,
The taste of terror rises to my pursed lips,
I feel sick.
The waves breaking; a stampede of horses
Stumbling over an innocent deer.
My eyes are freakishly wide,
I'm too scared to breathe.
I can't help it.
I shriek with fear,
I stumble over,
Then,
I drown . . .

Meg Davies (10)
Hartwell CE Primary School, Hartwell

The Wave

The wave sounds like a growling tiger
Ready to attack.
The ferocious wave tastes like
The fear and strength of the staring tiger.
The wave looks like it's leaping
For its innocent prey.
I could feel the terrible pain
Of the poor prey.

Robert Slaney (10)
Hartwell CE Primary School, Hartwell

The Wave

The wave looked like
A fire-breathing dragon
Awaking from its malodorous
Sleep!

The wave looked like
A dragon's
Scaly skin.

The wave sounded like
A dragon's fire
Hitting its hopeless prey.

You could taste
The saltwater
Flying into your mouth
Like a dragon's spit
Flying onto
Your pale face.

You could smell the
Salty water
Like a distorted
Dragon's odorous
Breath.

Tom Roe (10)
Hartwell CE Primary School, Hartwell

The Wave

The everlasting wave menacingly growled
Like an ogre ready to attack.
The dauntless surfer
Was a mouse tasting danger.

The giant wave ferociously rose
Like an audacious ogre,
Keen to destroy the helpless surfer.

The ogre-like wave could
Smell the hopeless surfer
From twenty miles away.
Would this be the end?

Stephanie Fisola Odukoya (10)
Hartwell CE Primary School, Hartwell

The Wave

The wave
Is like an
Ogre's powerful hand
Reaching out after
His innocent prey.
The roaring wave
Is like a
Ponderous ogre
Stalking his prey.
The ogre's
Disgusting breath
Is like
Rotten fish
Below the wave.

George Thumwood (10)
Hartwell CE Primary School, Hartwell

The Wave

The sound
Of the rumbling wave
Is like a tiger ready to attack
Its innocent prey.

I can taste
The fear and anger of the wave,
Which is like a staring tiger.

I can feel
The terrible pain of the
Wave's dramatic start.

Strength, anger and power,
It's the wave.

Lewis Johnson (10)
Hartwell CE Primary School, Hartwell

The Wave

The sinister wave menacingly rose like a crocodile
Leisurely opening its jaws to snap down on its prey.
Its prey,
Me.
I silently glide past on my vibrant surfboard,
Trying not to disturb the beast.
It holds its position; it starts coming down.
Down come the jaws,
I surf away faster and faster.
The crocodile's teeth come closer together,
Snap!
I narrowly escape, panting with fear.
The crocodile spits out spray,
Tearing me off my board
Into the dark water.

William Charter (10)
Hartwell CE Primary School, Hartwell

The Wave

The menacing wave
Looked like a deadly snake
Surreptitiously creeping
Up to its prey.
It was all over in an eclipse.
The defenceless prey was
Sliding across the deep, dark ocean.
The threatening species of Planet Earth
Compared to the small,
Defenceless prey below it.
The surfer was holding, holding,
Holding on for dear life,
As he had a 10% chance
Of survival against that, that thing,
That thing called the wave.

Travis Cook (10)
Hartwell CE Primary School, Hartwell

If I Was A Killer Whale

(Inspired by 'If I Had Wings' by Pie Corbett)

If I was a killer whale
I would gaze at a fish
Speeding past me like lightning.
A swarm of fish would stare at me.

If I was a killer whale,
I would sniff the coral and seaweed
Drifting about in the magnificent water.

If I was a killer whale
I would listen to the brilliant whales
Blowing their blowholes.
I would listen to the dolphins
Splashing in the calm water.

If I was a killer whale
I would swallow the saltiest fish
That were rainbow-coloured.

If I was a killer whale
I would whack the biggest rock that roughly.
I would feel the wind push the water
Across my smooth back
As I glided through the water.

George Irving (9)
Hartwell CE Primary School, Hartwell

If I Was A Millionaire
(Inspired by 'If I Had Wings' by Pie Corbett)

If I was a millionaire,
I would stare at the great pyramids of Giza,
I would stay at a five-star hotel.

If I was a millionaire,
I would sniff the exotic sweet scent of the spices of India,
I would dance to the Indian music.

If I was a millionaire,
I would gobble up every single piece of chocolate,
I would shop for the milkiest chocolate in Bruges.

If I was a millionaire,
I would surf the huge waves,
I would touch the soft sand of the Barrier Reef.

If I was a millionaire,
I would taste the world's most exotic fruits,
I would have a mango, banana and kiwi flavoured ice cream.

If I was a millionaire,
I would explore the world from top to bottom,
I would eat all sorts of different food
And see all sorts of amazing things.

Jessica Xupravati (9)
Hartwell CE Primary School, Hartwell

If I Was A Dog
(Inspired by 'If I Had Wings' by Pie Corbett)

If I was a dog,
I would gaze happily at my owner,
Then plod up to her, waiting for my well-earned dinner.

If I was a dog,
I would lie in my cosy, warm bed,
Stroking a smooth, fluffy, blue blanket sleepily.

If I was a dog,
I would listen to the wind ruffle
Through my short, golden hair.

If I was a dog,
I would gobble up my favourite
Succulent chunks of juicy meat.

If I was a dog,
I would get a whiff of the lovely scent
Of my dinner tempting me to gobble, gobble, gobble.

If I was a dog,
I would dream
Of happiness and love from my owner.

Maisie Randall (9)
Hartwell CE Primary School, Hartwell

A Baby Sister
(Inspired by 'If I Had Wings' by Pie Corbett)

If I had a baby sister,
I would gaze at her as she joyfully played
With her pink rattle with me.

If I had a baby sister,
I would help her softly toddle
Through the front room.

If I had a baby sister,
I could taste her runny nose
As she kissed me on my face.

If I had a baby sister,
I would touch her little soft hands
As she walked with me.

If I had a baby sister,
I could smell her delicious chocolate fingers
As she wiped them on me.

If I had a baby sister,
I would teach her how to talk and walk
And become just like me.

Beth Childs (9)
Hartwell CE Primary School, Hartwell

If I Was Magic
(Inspired by 'If I Had Wings' by Pie Corbett)

If I was magic,
I would see the Easter Island
And tickle the chins of the Easter Island statues.

If I was magic,
I would hear Michael Jackson
And listen to him singing 'Beat It'.

If I was magic,
I would smell a room full of gobstoppers,
Sweet, succulent and delicious.

If I was magic,
I would magic Jamie Oliver
And make him cook me the best fish and chips.

If I was magic,
I would hold the stars in my hand
And touch the planets with my feet.

If I was magic,
I would dream of riding the clouds
And flying the sea.

Thomas Heron (9)
Hartwell CE Primary School, Hartwell

If I Were A Star
(Inspired by 'If I Had Wings' by Pie Corbett)

If I were a star,
I would gaze at the planets orbiting around me
Like continuous spinning tops.

If I were a star,
I would hear the sun crackling
Like a blazing firework.

If I were a star,
I would stroke the tail of a comet,
As soft as a bear.

If I were a star,
I would taste the flames as they sneaked into my mouth,
Like smoke choking me.

If I were a star,
I would smell the burning fumes from rockets
Whizzing past me like a Formula 1 car lapping me.

If I were a star,
I would sit back and relax
And let the universe live around me.

Ellie Hansford (9)
Hartwell CE Primary School, Hartwell

If I Had Been In World War II
(Inspired by 'If I Had Wings' by Pie Corbett)

If I had been in World War II,
I would touch the rubble of a devastated house.
I would feel shrapnel's fingers, cold and dangerous.

If I had been in World War II,
I would be able to hear warnings, high and squeaky.
I would hear bombs crash-land on a house or road,
Making craters as deep as a mountain is tall.

If I had been in World War II,
I would smell smoke as her black hair coiled around me.
I could touch the silky band too.
I could smell fresh soil as we made
A safe and secure Anderson shelter.

If I had been in World War II,
I would see explosions
Like fireworks light up the night sky,
Cloudless and moonlit.
I would see shocked, upset and terrified people cry,
Homeless and frightened like rabbits being hunted.

Rebekah Potter (10)
Hartwell CE Primary School, Hartwell

If I Had Gills
(Inspired by 'If I Had Wings' by Pie Corbett)

If I had gills,
I would gaze at the baby sea horses bobbing up and down
Elegantly and carefully by my side.

If I had gills,
I would inhale the fresh salt that sways this way and that
Around me as I tear through the sea like a lightning strike.

If I had gills,
I would stroke the mighty great white whale
As he moodily sings the whale song
Powerfully swimming through the sea.

If I had gills,
I would nibble the slimy and putrid seaweed
That sways gently and silently
At the bottom of the seabed.

If I had gills,
I would listen to the sucking of the pufferfish on the rocks.
I would feel extraordinary.

Ryan Randall (9)
Hartwell CE Primary School, Hartwell

Aston Martin

(Inspired by 'If I Had Wings' by Pie Corbett)

If I had an Aston Martin,
I would rev it up to top,
I would see the cars zoom past me,
I would hear the V12 engine roar!

If I had an Aston Martin,
I would go out in it every day,
I would take it for a spin.

If I had an Aston Martin,
I would smell the new car fragrance,
I would gaze at it all day long,
I would feel proud that I owned one.

If I had an Aston Martin,
I would show it off at car shows,
I would clean it every day
So it was like a shiny diamond.

Louis Newcombe (9)
Hartwell CE Primary School, Hartwell

Wave

The gargantuan wave densely rises
From its extensive sleep,
Like a fierce wildcat awakening
From its slumber.

The underwater turbulence threatens
To vigorously tear me from my board,
Like a wildcat trying to separate
Its enemy from a carcass,
But I stay rooted to the board.

The roar is like a lion's majestic roar,
Striking fear into my heart.

The taste of fear is bitter and sour,
A wildcat's blood.
It suddenly breaks,
Crash!
Like a lion it pounces.
I narrowly escape.
Will it end?

James Morrison (10)
Hartwell CE Primary School, Hartwell

The Wave

The giant destroys everything around him,
He menacingly awakes,
Trying to catch his weak prey.
Feeling anxious at the monster,
Death is not far to those who dare approach it!
It feels like nature is against you!
Hear his malevolent roar,
He is as furious as a destructive bull
Ready to charge.
He is the monster,
Giant of the sea,
Ready to take out his enemies.
The taste of fear taunts you at every turn.
It is against you.
The giant's odorous stench is salty,
Toxic in every way.
Its name is the wave!

Thomas Sapwell (10)
Hartwell CE Primary School, Hartwell

The Wave

The wave
Surreptitiously rose
Like a tabby cat
Waiting, waiting to pounce murderously!
The rumbles
Of the darkest wave
Were like an earthquake,
Tantalising its defenceless prey.
The audacious surfer could
Taste fear in every direction.
Which direction would he turn?
The wave closed in rapidly,
Wherever he went.

James Gillard (10)
Hartwell CE Primary School, Hartwell

The Wave

The menacing wave
Growled at me
Like a starving cat,
Effortlessly fighting
For its hopeless prey.

Its audacious pounce
Was like when the
Gigantic wave breaks
Onto the abandoned warrior,
The wave secretly chuckling away.

I could taste the fear
That kept taunting me,
Never leaving my mind,
Never leaving me.
I could taste the fear
In every turn I took.
Then silence . . .
Silence.

Beattie Everatt (10)
Hartwell CE Primary School, Hartwell

The Wave

It approaches.
The wave,
Like a sinister cat,
Prowling closer.

It's ravenous.
The wave;
Like a crow,
It's illusive.

The wave,
It's bloodthirsty.
It's hungry like a malevolent bear.
The wave.

Joe Clarke (10)
Hartwell CE Primary School, Hartwell

The Wave

The relentless wave rises surreptitiously
Like a black bear raring up,
Ready to attack its helpless victim.

The man could taste death in the air
As the endless wave just wouldn't stop,
Though he distinctively tries to
Outrun the wave, like a mouse from a cat.

The man desperately tries to escape
The furious wave as it leaps down
Like a leopard jumping out of a tree.

Luke Addison (10)
Hartwell CE Primary School, Hartwell

The Giant

The rumbling sound of the wave
Menacingly grumbled,
Grumbled like a giant's tummy
Waiting, waiting for food.

The wave audaciously rose like a destructive hand,
Aiming to dominate me . . .
The wave broke,
Broke like a giant's hand crushing anyone,
Anyone who is in his path.

I can feel the vibration,
The vibration like a giant
Loudly stomping his foot down
On the rocky, hard ground.

I could smell the saltwater,
Has gone up my nose.
I could taste the fear,
Fear inside my dry mouth.

Amy Davies (10)
Hartwell CE Primary School, Hartwell

Elements

(Inspired by 'If I Had Wings' by Pie Corbett)

If I could control the elements,
I would smell the smoke from the fire blazing silently.

If I could control the elements,
I would hear the birds tweeting and I would move huge rocks,
It would be as loud as drums.

If I could control the elements,
I would touch the clouds,
I would feel as light as a feather
And the cloud would feel soft and cuddly.

If I could control the elements,
I would see Atlantis buried beneath the ocean,
The water would feel as cold as ice.

If I could control the elements,
I would taste the water tickling my tongue.

Charlotte Evans (9)
Hartwell CE Primary School, Hartwell

The Wave

A giant wave
Awakes sluggishly from its slumber
To catch its prey,
That had challenged it
Like a moth to a flame.

You could feel his undefeatable anger
In every drop of his saliva,
That held more anger
Than an erupting volcano.

The exuberant wave
Malevolently growls,
Like a cat in distress.

Is it a monster?
No!
It is . . . the wave.

William Addy (10)
Hartwell CE Primary School, Hartwell

55

If I Had A Time Machine
(Inspired by 'If I Had Wings' by Pie Corbett)

If I had a time machine,
I would listen to the echoing sound
Of it slicing through the interesting time.

If I had a time machine,
I would go and see the hairy, scary Gruffalo
From the future.

If I had a time machine,
I would go to see the Vikings
And swing the heavy metal axe around my head.

If I had a time machine,
I would choke on the disgusting smoke
Of the Great Fire of London in 1666.

If I had a time machine,
I would smell the blazing flames
After the bombing of World War II.

Marley Nisic (9)
Hartwell CE Primary School, Hartwell

The Wave

The surreptitious wave
Menacingly grew,
Like a clawed, bony hand
Grabbing,
Grabbing the hopeless surfer.
The wave
Grew and grew until
The wave was towering,
Towering over the audacious surfer.
The wave
Was taunting him
Like a tiger ready to pounce.
There were massive vibrations,
It was like an earthquake.
Just then,
Silence . . .
Its name is the wave.

James Cunningham (10)
Hartwell CE Primary School, Hartwell

Chocolate
(Inspired by 'If I Had Wings' by Pie Corbett)

If I had all the chocolate in the world,
I would make a house out of it.
I would gobble it when I wanted
And I would never feel sick.

If I had all the chocolate in the world,
I would melt the luxurious, sweet, creamy
Chocolate in my mouth.

If I had all the chocolate in the world,
I would carve the Man United team
In the chocolate
And eat one player every day.

If I had all the chocolate in the world,
I would give to other people.

If I had all the chocolate in the world,
I would share it with all my friends
And the whole school, including teachers.

Libby Cook (9)
Hartwell CE Primary School, Hartwell

The Wave

The menacing wave looks like a deadly snake,
Surreptitiously creeping up to its defenceless prey.
Soon, the wave aggressively towers over the terrified surfer,
Like a snake preparing to destroy its helpless prey.
Suddenly the wave broke
Into what seemed a full eclipse,
Like a vigorous snake engulfing its prey.

Lewis Anderson (10)
Hartwell CE Primary School, Hartwell

The Wave

The wave looked like a frustrated ogre
Gradually awaking from his black sleep.
The merciless wave
Vigorously rumbles
Like an ogre
Carelessly grumbling at its victim.

Matthew Ward (10)
Hartwell CE Primary School, Hartwell

Swoosh, Splash, Crash

Swoosh, splash, crash,
Crashing waves tower over me, as high as a skyscraper,
Swoosh, splash, crash,
Hands of icy water grab my feet and pull me under,
Swoosh, splash, crash,
Waves all around throwing themselves all over,
Swoosh, splash, crash,
As shimmering as a newborn star in the night sky,
Swoosh, splash, crash,
As blue as crystals shining in a cave,
Swoosh, splash, crash,
As fast as a cheetah going for its prey,
Swoosh, splash, crash,
When the wave hits the water I get a spray of water,
Swoosh, splash, crash,
Water belting down the waves at the speed of light,
Swoosh, splash, crash,
So powerful but fast it hits the water surface,
Swoosh, splash, crash,
Water dancing in the wind,
Swoosh, splash, crash,
The waves take me home to the sandy shore with one final
Swoosh, splash, crash.

Ella May O'Hare (10)
High Street CP School, Winsford

The Crashing Waves

Waves of icy water crashing, smashing;
Roaring at the boats,
Throwing itself over Mount Fuji as it hits the rocks,
Like a racing, raging roller coaster.
Gigantic hands of icy water grab my freezing feet as it pulls me under.
The waves crash; smash into the boats,
Extreme crystal-blue fists of water crash into Mount Fuji.
Waves are killers.
Beating the boats,
The water smashes the boats.
Water as fast as a cheetah,
Jumps into the boats.
Waves are killers.
Waves are like lions hunting for prey.
Prancing at the boats like its prey
Waves sprint to the boats getting ready to attack
The stormy sea jumps to the boats and crushes them.
Waves are killers.

Ethan Presland (10)
High Street CP School, Winsford

The Waterfall

As fast as lightning the churning torrent of water shimmered down the
glittering stream,
The water smashed and crashed on the bank like a stampede of white
horses,
When it reached the cliff edge the water cascaded over the edge like a
swooping bird,
As the water droplets experienced weightlessness, they barged into each
other,
Viciously the water splashed like an explosion at the bottom of the waterfall,
At the bottom of the waterfall the water sprinted through the rocks, agile and
twisting them it reached the wide, deep blue sea,
Once in the sea the water starts its cycle up into the clouds and it starts all
over again.

Charlie Oliver (11)
High Street CP School, Winsford

The Horse In The Waves

Leap, splash, leap!
Goes the horse in the waves,
It jumps over all the hazards that come in its way
Like a hunt chasing its prey,
It stomps, skips, prances!
Like its kin in a dressage test,
It is a twinkling jewel in the sea,
A beauty of all radiant beauties,
Rear, skip, trot!
The horse in the waves,
Is nearing its final destination,
It stops shining a brilliant white,
It is now a boring blue,
For it is now a small child,
A young foal!
Ready to once again start again,
As a large graceful wave,
It crashes, breaks and falls;
Once again begins its life as a child.

Emily Hall (10)
High Street CP School, Winsford

The Evil Wave

Humongous large waves hang over
ready to drown their prey like a tiger pouncing on its meal.
Fishermen cry for help on their small battered boats.
Mount Fuji watches the wave still standing
taking its visitors under.
Soaring birds have no room to fly,
the towering wave leaves them no room.
Splashing, crashing, clashing
The immense waves take down the boats and
swallows them in one gulp and ashores them on dry land to comfort.
As the splashing, crashing, clashing waves rest their
evilness for another day.

Ellie Hulse (10)
High Street CP School, Winsford

The Vast Wave

It drops like a hawk hunts, slaying the air, *slap!*
Clout! It hits the surface.
Crashing and soaring through the boats.
Whilst Mt Fuji watches the torture.
It gains boats
It's the vast wave.
It's a white lion hunting for his prey.
It's fast and bold there for nothing will protest with it.
Roaring and disputing Mt Fuji
Tracking and stalking, it watches over the crystals.
Making sure it's king of its glorious home.
It's the vast wave
It's a mustang pulling the god of sea.
Everything against it is defenceless.
Its job is complete, but there it goes again.
Only that this time it's much, much more immense
It's the vastest wave over!

Dane Lee Rigby (11)
High Street CP School, Winsford

Big Waves At Mount Fuji

That's the sound as the extreme crystal-blue
waves kick the sea at Mount Fuji.
People on their boats are shivering with
fear as they bounce up and down like a
ten-year-old boy bungee-jumping.
The people hit the waves.
They are dragged into the frozen sea
with a great big *splash!*
So now people who last went on the
mind-twisty sea know the innocent poor people
who last went on the sea and gave away their
previous tragic lives to the sea.

But the news has happened, the gigantic
wave has never come back to Mount Fuji.
So now there will be no more fear as the
wave has never come back to Mount Fuji.

Joshua Shaw (10)
High Street CP School, Winsford

61

The Killer Waves

The huge, terrifying waves were bigger than Mount Fuji.
They were called killer waves.
The ginormous waves cover the shadowy water.
Waves are beating up the tiny boats as they pass.
The water pulls the boats under with its hands of icy water.
The water is as blue as the sky but it's a killer munching on fish; boats as
they sprint into the starving waves.
The water's a killer, watch out for him.
If the waves see you don't look back at them.
Watch out, he's coming for you!
As Mount Fuji watches in the distance there's nothing to do.
When the killer waves come.

Nathan Symington Dunbavin (10)
High Street CP School, Winsford

The Flowing Monster

The flowing monster is an endless time machine.
A raging river, as scary as a dragon's lair.

It takes you under in one huge splash,
As if you were being pulled down,
Whilst you're freezing in the icy pool,
Which is the river.

The flowing monster is an endless time machine,
A raging river, as scary as a dragon's lair,
I am the raging river,
I am the beast of the water.

Callum Ian McCormack (10)
High Street CP School, Winsford

Smashing And Crashing

Smashing and crashing the waves march like a soldier
towards the shore, blue like a shimmering sapphire
twinkling droplets catch the sun,
crystal water, cold as ice.

Connor Done (10)
High Street CP School, Winsford

The Floating Wave

The waves were as thin as a sharp knife.
Powerful waves are like a rolling, roaring roller coaster
rushing to get past the sharp icicles.
Water is a sheet of silky blue, soft blanket.
As thin waves crash, smash, flash you see
sparkling little icicles in the water.
Mount Fuji has its mysterious eyes on
you as you sail across the ferocious water.

Katie Rowland (10)
High Street CP School, Winsford

Wacky Water

Ferociously the torrent of water ran down the magnificent stream as if it was
being chased,
Banks were being smashed as if they were punched by a boxer,
Magnificent water was a blue sheet among the swaying trees.

Wonderful water was racing the fish towards the lake,
Twisting and turning among the giant reeds.

Reaching the lake a beautiful scene was revealed,
A magnificent magical place, there was splashing and swirling everywhere,
It was brilliant.

Jamie John Young (10)
High Street CP School, Winsford

Diamond Water

Water sparkles all day long;
When it turns dark.
The sharks come out to play;
The sea goes silent;
All you can hear is the pitter-patter of your own heart.
Water is a diamond, it sparkles in the sunlight;
When it turns dark.
It dances in the dark, it makes crashing, pounding waves.
Hitting the watery surface.

Callum Parkinson (11)
High Street CP School, Winsford

Mighty Waves

Mighty waves splash fiercely over the rough edge of the waterfall.

Water lashing out like thunder across the never-ending river.

Bubbling dangerously, the ice-cold waves smacking over each other, swirling across the bank.

As the sharp, crystal-clear waves slide over the rough, decaying edge the tiny fish fight for survival.

The water and waves calm down and the waves swish softly.

Ellena Phillips (10)
High Street CP School, Winsford

The Big Wave

Big as a mountain racing through the sea, a wave is coming.
Crashing; gushing in the air, splashing, splashing always crashing
Just crashing; splashing, gobbling up all the fish, just in one.
Sucking up boats, leaving a trail of wreckage.
Sneaking like a cheetah behind boats, waiting for them to turn around.
Then pound! The boats are gone, always sneaking; always pounding
Sucking up boats just like a baby, ready to grow.
Mount Fuji seeing what it's doing can't move but can see.

Iaian James Mahon (10)
High Street CP School, Winsford

The Ferocious Waves

Waves are like a hand of icy water roaring like a lion
gushing over the boats.
Water is crashing into the side of the boat;
Gushing through the side of the boat - roars like a lorry.
It's crashing down into the boat; however
Mount Fuji sits there; ferocious waves
are crashing the boats that go past him.

James Maddock (10)
High Street CP School, Winsford

The Big Wave

As the beautiful crystal-clear waves
crashed against the villagers' wooden well-crafted boats,
All of the helpless, innocent people of the village
ran away as fast as a speeding bullet for higher land,
Not caring about the poor, innocent
people on the pointed, strong boats.

Lauren Percival
High Street CP School, Winsford

Have You Ever Seen . . . ?

Have you ever seen . . .
A giraffe with ten tails?
A tiger who is scared of snails?
A student who never fails?
A man eating twenty whales?
I don't think you have heard these tales . . .

Or have you seen a zebra with spots?
Or a human who eats garden pots?
A lion who is made up of dots?
Or a boy who speaks the language of Lots?
I think my imagination has gone off the trot . . .

Have you seen a tortoise that speeds?
Or a mammoth that was found in Leeds?
A hyena made of reeds?
Or a gardener who adores weeds?
I think my thinking requires vital needs . . .

I am a crazy thinker,
And my brain does not tinker,
I am a confident winker,
No wonder I received minus ten out of ten in common sense!

Achal Srivastav (10)
Homefield Prep School, Sutton

Infestation

Scales are red,
Eyes are green,
Claws are sharp,
Doesn't care about hygiene.
Over the hill,
Red creatures are spread,
Far from human,
The disease has spread.
It swarms into cities, towns and homes,
Kills all life,
'Cept the useful,
Inside of which it roams.
It feasts on organs,
Cracks the skull,
You better run,
Or turn into the hunt.

Oliver Hilton (10)
Homefield Prep School, Sutton

The Waterfall

The waterfall flows like an upright stream.
Its azure-blue water shooting down in a beam.
Its amazing gracefulness as it slowly falls down.
It's like Rapunzel's golden hair falling into her crown.
The pure, sweet water is fresh and new.
If there were no waterfalls I don't know what I would do.

Michael Banh & Maiann Lenhardt-Vu (10)
Homefield Prep School, Sutton

The Sea

Watch the tranquil seashore
Then dive deep to the sea floor
Watch the fish swimming by
But if you see a shark, stand by.

A whale sings a song, deep into the ocean
A song of joy and devotion
You see the fishing nets by the waves
Very sad like church graves.

The sea is aqua-blue
The perfect place for me and you.

Ash Sood (10)
Homefield Prep School, Sutton

Autumn

Apples falling from the trees
Littering the orchard, carrying their secret inside.

The blackberries hang from the
Hedgerows dripping shiny drops of juice.

The horse chestnuts fall to the ground,
Carrying their shiny bright jewel inside.

The acorns are dropping
Squirrels are all gathering hurriedly
For their winter stock.

Alice Holmes (9)
Ingleby Arncliffe CE Primary School, Northallerton

Fruits Of Autumn

Red and green apples
Juicy and fresh, hiding
Their glistening secret

Elderberries hang like
Beads of jet in juicy
Sweet, black clusters

Tall, majestic, soft
Bulrushes standing like
Buildings guarding the lakeside

Spiky horse chestnuts
Crack open and
Show their glossy brown conkers

Vivid orange Chinese lanterns
Filling the borders
With vibrant colours

Golden brown plums
Hanging like giant teardrops
Falling into eager hands

The blackberries hanging
From the trees bursting
With juicy flavour.

Emma Bailey (10)
Ingleby Arncliffe CE Primary School, Northallerton

Fruits Of Autumn

It's time to gather fruit
Red and green apples hanging like giant teardrops,
Apples falling into eager hands,
The smell of apple pie, yum-yum!

Glossy brown conkers blown down by the wind,
Thud! Thud! They fall,
Children playing with conkers, dawn 'til dusk,
Hard and spiky shell prickly to touch. *Ouch!*

JJ Wannell (7)
Ingleby Arncliffe CE Primary School, Northallerton

The Joys Of Autumn

As I stroll along the path I'm surrounded by fog,
Dying trees all around me and mossy logs,
Blueberries on trees, itching to fall,
A tiny blue gem like a flavoursome ball,

Plums are a gorgeous little treat,
Pink or red, sticky and sweet,
Elderberry juice staining my lips,
As well as raspberries, blackberries and rosehips,

Shells are cracking, peering at the light,
As the conkers are ready and ripe,
Apples and pears hanging from trees,
Like bombs waiting for release,

Eating roast dinners big and heart-warming,
Old leaves dying, new leaves forming.

Murdo MacColl (10)
Ingleby Arncliffe CE Primary School, Northallerton

All About Me!

L ove is what I think to many things
    these are just a few, written in the letters of my name.

A nimals is one I love, if they tweet,
    cheep, fly or crawl, I do not care, I love them all.

U nlimited chocolate I sure do love
    Cadburys, Rolo, Aero and more, I sure would take it if it was at my door.

R eading is also what I love to do
    to spell and learn all new words.

E xcited is what I love to be
    for many things I'm looking forward to
    the only feeling I get then is excitement.

N ight stars I love to look at,
    they hover in the dark blue sky at night.

These are the things I love!

Lauren Head (10)
Ingrave Johnstone CE (VA) Primary School, Brentwood

69

My Magical Box

In my box I have many wonderful things -

A scary mouse
A pink house

Doors that swing
Bells that ring

Banana smoothies
Funny movies

A Christmas tree
Santa's grotto key

A leaking pen
My secret den

My box is hidden in a secret place
So don't go looking for it because it's tided up with a lace!

Roxanne Faye Brown (11)
Ingrave Johnstone CE (VA) Primary School, Brentwood

True Friendship

Friendship is like a flower.
Friendship is like a good person who will never hurt you.
Friendship is like a rose that just gets prettier.

Friendship is like a very good book.
Friendship is like a very good CD.
Friendship is like a house and key that only match each other.

Friendship is like love that never ends.
Friendship is like a bed of flowers that just gets nicer day by day.
Friendship is like your mum and dad who stay with you forever.

Friendship is like cute kittens.
Friendship is like your favourite cake.
Friendship is you and I, best friends forever.

Liberty Nicole Lynch (10)
Ingrave Johnstone CE (VA) Primary School, Brentwood

Sound Of Music

Flute is a high-pitched sound
It travels here and all around
A flute is a high-pitched sound.

Saxophone has a jazzy rhythm
It trumps here and everywhere
It's a jazzy rhythm.

Trumpet is loud and hard to play
It has a lovely sound.

Piano has a wonderful sound
When you play it fluently.

Leonard Stannard (10)
Ingrave Johnstone CE (VA) Primary School, Brentwood

Jimbo

Jimbo is a friend
A very nice friend
I cuddle him tight
When it is night
Jimbo is my buddy
He sometimes gets muddy
But I don't care, he is my
Bubby!

Allanah Murphy (10)
Ingrave Johnstone CE (VA) Primary School, Brentwood

Surf!

I am off surfing, I am up like a lark, I hope I don't bump into a shark.
The waves crash on the beach, so for my surfboard I reach.
Jump up on my board, heading out to sea,
I'm looking for the biggest wave to carry me,
I'm trying not to fall and I can hear the seagulls' call.
The slab takes me back to land
Then I see a crab hide in the sand.
Then I see a great big shark and swim to shore before it's dark.

Sam Dunn (10)
Ingrave Johnstone CE (VA) Primary School, Brentwood

I Love My Mummy

I've loved my mummy from when I was in her tummy,
She is my best mate and I think she is great!
I know she's a winner when she cooks me my dinner,
She makes me laugh when I'm in the bath!
I love her so much when she cleans out my guinea pig hutch,
She gets in a muddle but I give her a great big cuddle!

Megan Meany (10)
Ingrave Johnstone CE (VA) Primary School, Brentwood

Sports

S wimming is a sport that includes water.
P olo is a sport that includes horses.
O rienteering has a lot of running in it.
R ugby is a tough game.
T ennis includes a ball and a tennis racket.

Emma Greenwood (8)
Ingrave Johnstone CE (VA) Primary School, Brentwood

Gills
(Inspired by 'If I Had Wings' by Pie Corbett)

If I had gills
I would float like a turtle in the shimmering lake water.

If I had gills
I would marry a handsome merman.

If I had gills
I would live in the shimmering seawater near a lakeside tree.

If I had gills
I would build a mansion under the blue sea made of the Titanic and meet
the king and queen.

If I had gills
I would have a delightful burger with a greedy crab, a moaning squid and a
spontaneous sponge.

Caitlyn Hetem (9)
Longlands Primary School & Nursery, Broxbourne

Gills

(Inspired by 'If I Had Wings' by Pie Corbett)

If I had gills
I would watch clownfish juggle at the sea circus.

If I had gills
I would be in business with a loan shark.

If I had gills
I would build a mansion under the sea
and call my octopus friend over for tea.

If I had gills
I would hunt down the exotic treasures
that lurk in the deep blue sea.

If I had gills
I would make a tune up with a tuna on a tuba.

Jordan Tadgell (9)
Longlands Primary School & Nursery, Broxbourne

Gills

(Inspired by 'If I Had Wings' by Pie Corbett)

If I had gills
I would swim with a mermaid.

If I had gills
I would play a game with a swordfish.

If I had gills
I would meet a Great White shark.

If I had gills
I would swim like the wind.

If I had gills
I would play football with a jellyfish.

Alexandra Taylor (9)
Longlands Primary School & Nursery, Broxbourne

Gills

(Inspired by 'If I Had Wings' by Pie Corbett)

If I had gills
I would race a marlin.

If I had gills
I would have a sword fight with a swordfish.

If I had gills
I would defend the sharks from poachers.

If I had gills
I would wrestle a hammerhead.

If I had gills
I would play chess with a blue-tipped shark.

Dane Gonzalez (10)
Longlands Primary School & Nursery, Broxbourne

Gills

(Inspired by 'If I Had Wings' by Pie Corbett)

If I had gills
I would eat a wriggling tadpole.

If I had gills
I would live under the ocean roof forever.

If I had gills
I would marry a fierce swordfish.

If I had gills
I would go to the beach to see the glistening sunset.

The water will shine to me.

Leighanna Smith (9)
Longlands Primary School & Nursery, Broxbourne

Animal Riddle

S ome fear him.
Others use P ens to hit him.
As sw I ft as a swooping owl
As D elicate as glass
Sup E rb at speed
R aging with venom.

Duke Ansah (9)
Longlands Primary School & Nursery, Broxbourne

Gills

(Inspired by 'If I Had Wings' by Pie Corbett)

If I had gills
I would marry a swordfish.

If I had gills
I would build a mansion and make a sea cart.

If I had gills
I would introduce myself to a Great White.

If I had gills
I would play darts with a jellyfish.

Ryan Phillips (9)
Longlands Primary School & Nursery, Broxbourne

Gills

(Inspired by 'If I Had Wings' by Pie Corbett)

If I had gills
I would touch the deepest part of the ocean.

If I had gills
I would race a swift tiger shark.

If I had gills
I would watch the shiny, deep blue water glistening all day.

If I had gills
I would build a crusty cabin out of shipwrecks.

Gaia Natoli (9)
Longlands Primary School & Nursery, Broxbourne

Gills
(Inspired by 'If I Had Wings' by Pie Corbett)

If I had gills
I would blend in the seaweed forest.

If I had gills
I would dine on tuna every day.

If I had gills
I would make friends with a loyal swordfish.

Tobi Adetola (9)
Longlands Primary School & Nursery, Broxbourne

Animal Riddle

Hungry
Camouflaged in the grassland
Ready to spring out
The zebra as foolish as a donkey
Waiting to be eaten
With jaws as strong as a hippo
He pounces and kills.

Harry Smith (9)
Longlands Primary School & Nursery, Broxbourne

Animal Riddle

As swift as a S weeping owl.
As deadly as a bottle of P oison.
With eyes as black as the n I ght.
He crawls out in the D ark.
With fangs as sharp as sharp as kniv E s.
He creeps down the R oad.

Safa Khan (10)
Longlands Primary School & Nursery, Broxbourne

Animal Riddle

Legs as hairy a S a moustache.
P erfect shiny cobweb.
With eyes as black as n I ght.
D angerous scissor fangs
drip with d E adly poison.
The fly neve R saw it coming.

Francesca Buckle (9)
Longlands Primary School & Nursery, Broxbourne

Animal Riddle

Eye S like burnt fire.
Fangs as shar P as a knife.
Deadly as a l i on.
Fangs D rip with poisonous venom.
Hook E d legs.
Swift as a high-speed t R ain.

Chloe Hickling (9)
Longlands Primary School & Nursery, Broxbourne

Animal Riddle

As swift as a S wooping owl
As deadly as P oison
Mud f I end
More D elicate than egg shells
Hunts for his pr E y with venom like a loaded gun
Fangs as sha R p as claws.

Alfie Meader (9)
Longlands Primary School & Nursery, Broxbourne

Animal Riddle

S neakier than a mouse.
As cree P y as a horror movie.
As ha I ry as your head.
Its web is as D elicate as a feather.
It hunts for its pr E y like a cheetah.
C R awling like a baby.

Sinead Wines (9)
Longlands Primary School & Nursery, Broxbourne

Animal Riddle

S hooting its gleaming cobwebs,
He collects P earls.
As sw I ft as a train he catches flies.
D ancing on the silver cobweb.
H E sucks a fly's blood.
He always moves f R om place to place.

Charlotte Reeves (9)
Longlands Primary School & Nursery, Broxbourne

Animal Riddle

His eyes are as black as a S hadow
He catches P rey on his web
K I llers
His swor D fangs drip with venom
As sn E aky as a ghost
As deadly as elect R ic.

Ryan Coomes (9)
Longlands Primary School & Nursery, Broxbourne

Featured Author:

Maddie Stewart

Maddie is a children's writer, poet and author who currently lives in Coney Island, Northern Ireland.

Maddie has 5 published children's books, 'Cinders', 'Hal's Sleepover', 'Bertie Rooster', 'Peg' and 'Clever Daddy'. Maddie uses her own unpublished work to provide entertaining, interactive poems and rhyming stories for use in her workshops with children when she visits schools, libraries, arts centres and book festivals.

Favourites are 'Silly Billy, Auntie Millie' and 'I'm a Cool, Cool Kid'. Maddie works throughout Ireland from her home in County Down. She is also happy to work from a variety of bases in England. She has friends and family, with whom she regularly stays, in Leicester, Bedford, London and Ashford (Kent). Maddie's workshops are aimed at 5-11-year-olds. Check out Maddie's website for all her latest news and free poetry resources **www.maddiestewart.com**.

Read on to pick up some fab writing tips!

NONSENSE WORKSHOP

IF YOU FIND SILLINESS FUN,
YOU WILL LOVE NONSENSE POEMS.
NONSENSE POEMS MIGHT DESCRIBE SILLY THINGS,
OR PEOPLE, OR SITUATIONS,
OR, ANY COMBINATION OF THE THREE.

For example:

When I got out of bed today,
both my arms had run away.
I sent my feet to fetch them back.
When they came back, toe in hand
I realised what they had planned.
They'd made the breakfast I love most,
buttered spider's eggs on toast.

**One way to find out if you enjoy nonsense poems
is to start with familiar nursery rhymes.
Ask your teacher to read them out,
putting in the names of some children in your class.**

Like this: Troy and Jill went up the hill
to fetch a pail of water.
Troy fell down
and broke his crown
and Jill came tumbling after.

If anyone is upset at the idea of using their name, then don't use it.

Did you find this fun?

**Now try changing a nursery rhyme.
Keep the rhythm and the rhyme style, but invent a silly situation.**

Like this: Hickory Dickory Dare
a pig flew up in the air.
The clouds above
gave him a shove
Hickory Dickory Dare.

Or this: Little Miss Mabel
sat at her table
eating a strawberry pie
but a big, hairy beast
stole her strawberry feast
and made poor little Mabel cry.

How does your rhyme sound if you put your own name in it?

**Another idea for nonsense poems is to pretend letters are people
and have them do silly things.**

For example:

Mrs A	Mrs B	Mrs C
Lost her way	Dropped a pea	Ate a tree

**To make your own 'Silly People Poem', think of a word to use.
To show you an example, I will choose the word 'silly'.
Write your word vertically down the left hand side of your page.
Then write down some words which rhyme
with the sound of each letter.**

S mess, dress, Bess, chess, cress
I eye, bye, sky, guy, pie, sky
L sell, bell, shell, tell, swell, well
L " " " " " " (" means the same as written above)
Y (the same words as those rhyming with I)

Use your rhyming word lists to help you make up your poem.

Mrs S made a mess
Mrs I ate a pie
Mrs L rang a bell
Mrs L broke a shell
Mrs Y said 'Bye-bye.'

You might even make a 'Silly Alphabet' by using
all the letters of the alphabet.

It is hard to find rhyming words for all the letters.
H, X and W are letters which are hard to match with rhyming words.
I'll give you some I've thought of:

H - cage, stage, wage (close but not perfect)
X - flex, specs, complex, Middlesex
W - trouble you, chicken coop, bubble zoo

However, with nonsense poems, you can use nonsense words.
You can make up your own words.

To start making up nonsense words you could
try mixing dictionary words together.
Let's make up some nonsense animals.

Make two lists of animals. (You can include birds and fish as well.)

Your lists can be as long as you like. These are lists I made:

elephant	kangaroo
tiger	penguin
lizard	octopus
monkey	chicken

Now use the start of an animal on one list and substitute
it for the start of an animal from your other list.

I might use the start of oct/opus ... oct and substitute it for the end of l/izard
to give me a new nonsense animal ... an octizard.
I might swap the start of monk/ey ... monk with the end of kang/aroo
To give me another new nonsense animal ... a monkaroo.

What might a monkaroo look like? What might it eat?

You could try mixing some food words in the same way,
to make up nonsense foods.

cabbage	potatoes
lettuce	parsley
bacon	crisps

Cribbage, bacley, and lettatoes are some nonsense foods
made up from my lists.

Let's see if I can make a nonsense poem about my monkaroo.

My monkaroo loves bacley.
He'll eat lettatoes too
But his favourite food is cribbage
Especially if it's blue.

Would you like to try and make up your own nonsense poem?

**Nonsense words don't have to be a combination of dictionary words.
They can be completely 'made up'.
You can use nonsense words to write nonsense sonnets,
or list poems or any type of poem you like.**

Here is a poem full of nonsense words:

I melly micked a turdle
and flecked a pendril's tum.
I plotineyed a shugat
and dracked a pipin's plum.

**Ask your teacher to read it putting in some children's names instead
of the first I, and he or she instead of the second I.**

Did that sound funny?

You might think that nonsense poems are just silly and not for the serious poet.
However poets tend to love language. Making up your own words is a natural
part of enjoying words and sounds and how they fit together. Many poets love the
freedom nonsense poems give them. Lots and lots of very famous poets have written
nonsense poems. I'll name some: **Edward Lear**, **Roger McGough**, **Lewis Carroll**,
Jack Prelutsky and **Nick Toczek**. Can you or your teacher think of any more?
For help with a class nonsense poem or to find more nonsense nursery rhymes look
on my website, **www.maddiestewart.com**. Have fun! Maddie Stewart.

POETIC TECHNIQUES

HERE IS a SELECTION OF POETRY TECHNIQUES WITH EXaMPLES

Metaphors & Similes

A *metaphor* is when you describe your subject *as* something else, for example:
'Winter is a cruel master leaving the servants in a bleak wilderness'
whereas a *simile* describes your subject *like* something else i.e.
'His blue eyes are like ice-cold puddles' or 'The flames flickered like eyelashes'.

Personification

This is to simply give a personality to something that is not human, for example
'Fear spreads her uneasiness around' or 'Summer casts down her warm sunrays'.

Imagery

To use words to create mental pictures of what you are trying to convey,
your poem should awaken the senses and make the reader
feel like they are in that poetic scene …
'The sky was streaked with pink and red as shadows
cast across the once-golden sand'.
'The sea gently lapped the shore as the palm trees rustled softly
in the evening breeze'.

Assonance & Alliteration

Alliteration uses a repeated constant sound and this effect can be quite striking:
'Smash, slippery snake slithered sideways'.
Assonance repeats a significant vowel or vowel sound to create an impact:
'The pool looked cool'.

Repetition

By repeating a significant word the echo effect can be a very powerful way of enhancing an emotion or point your poem is putting across.
'The blows rained down, down,
Never ceasing,
Never caring
About the pain,
The pain'.

Onomatopoeia

This simply means you use words that sound like the noise you are describing, for example 'The rain *pattered* on the window' or 'The tin can *clattered* up the alley'.

Rhythm & Metre

The *rhythm* of a poem means 'the beat', the sense of movement you create. The placing of punctuation and the use of syllables affect the *rhythm* of the poem. If your intention is to have your poem read slowly, use double, triple or larger syllables and punctuate more often, where as if you want to have a fast-paced read use single syllables, less punctuation and shorter sentences.
If you have a regular rhythm throughout your poem this is known as *metre*.

Enjambment

This means you don't use punctuation at the end of your line, you simply let the line flow on to the next one. It is commonly used and is a good word to drop into your homework!

Tone & Lyric

The poet's intention is expressed through their *tone*. You may feel happiness, anger, confusion, loathing or admiration for your poetic subject. Are you criticising or praising? How you feel about your topic will affect your choice of words and therefore your *tone*. For example 'I *loved* her', 'I *cared* for her', 'I *liked* her'.
If you write the poem from a personal view or experience this is referred to as a *lyrical* poem. A good example of a lyrical poem is Seamus Heaney's 'Mid-term Break' or any sonnet!

All About Shakespeare

TRY THIS FUN QUIZ WITH YOUR FAMILY, FRIENDS OR EVEN IN CLASS!

1. Where was Shakespeare born?

....

2. Mercutio is a character in which Shakepeare play?

....

3. Which monarch was said to be 'quite a fan' of his work?

....

4. How old was he when he married?

....

5. What is the name of the last and 'only original' play he wrote?

....

6. What are the names of King Lear's three daughters?

....

7. Who is Anne Hathaway?

....

8. Which city is the play 'Othello' set in?

....

9. Can you name 2 of Shakespeare's 17 comedies?

....

10. 'This day is call'd the feast of Crispian: He that outlives this day, and comes safe home, Will stand a tip-toe when this day is nam'd, and rouse him at the name of Crispian' is a quote from which play?

....

11. Leonardo DiCaprio played Romeo in the modern day film version of Romeo and Juliet. Who played Juliet in the movie?

....

12. Three witches famously appear in which play?

....

13. Which famous Shakespearean character is Eric in the image to the left?

....

14. What was Shakespeare's favourite poetic form?

....

Answers are printed on the last page of the book, good luck!

If you would rather try the quiz online, you can do so at www.youngwriters.co.uk.

POETRY ACTIVITY

WORD SOUP

**To help you write a poem, or even a story,
on any theme, you should create word soup!**

If you have a theme or subject for your poem, base your word soup on it.
If not, don't worry, the word soup will help you find a theme.

To start your word soup you need ingredients:

- Nouns (names of people, places, objects, feelings, i.e. Mum, Paris, house, anger)
- Colours
- Verbs ('doing words', i.e. kicking, laughing, running, falling, smiling)
- Adjectives (words that describe nouns, i.e. tall, hairy, hollow, smelly, angelic)

We suggest at least 5 of each from the above list, this will make sure your word soup
has plenty of choice. Now, if you have already been given a theme or title for your
poem, base your ingredients on this. If you have no idea what to write about,
write down whatever you like, or ask a teacher or family member to give you
a theme to write about.

Making Word Soup

Next, you'll need a sheet of paper.
Cut it into at least 20 pieces. Make sure the pieces are big enough to write your ingredients on, one ingredient on each piece of paper.
Write your ingredients on the pieces of paper.
Shuffle the pieces of paper and put them all in a box or bowl
- something you can pick the paper out of without looking at the words.
Pick out 5 words to start and use them to write your poem!

Example:

Our theme is winter. Our ingredients are:
- Nouns: snowflake, Santa, hat, Christmas, snowman.
- Colours: blue, white, green, orange, red.
- Verbs: ice-skating, playing, laughing, smiling, wrapping.
- Adjectives: cold, tall, fast, crunchy, sparkly.

Our word soup gave us these 5 words:
snowman, red, cold, hat, fast and our poem goes like this:

It's a *cold* winter's day,
My nose and cheeks are *red*
As I'm outside, building my *snowman*,
I add a *hat* and a carrot nose to finish,
I hope he doesn't melt too *fast*!

Tip: add more ingredients to your word soup
and see how many different poems you can write!

Tip: if you're finding it hard to write a poem with
the words you've picked, swap a word with another one!

Tip: try adding poem styles and techniques,
such as assonance or haiku to your soup for an added challenge!

SCRIBBLER!

If you enjoy creative writing then you'll love our magazine, Scribbler!,
the fun and educational magazine for 7-11-year-olds that works alongside
Key Stage 2 National Literacy Strategy Learning Objectives.
*For further information visit **www.youngwriters.co.uk**.*

Grammar Fun
Our resident dinosaur Bernard helps to improve writing skills from punctuation to spelling.

Nessie's Workshop
Each issue Nessie explains a style of writing and sets an exercise for you to do. Previous workshops include the limerick, haiku and shape poems.

Awesome Author
Read all about past and present authors. Previous Awesome Authors include Roald Dahl, William Shakespeare and Ricky Gervais!

Once Upon a Time …
Lord Oscar starts a story … it's your job to finish it. Our favourite wins a writing set.

Guest Author
A famous author drops by and answers some of our in-depth questions, while donating a great prize to give away. Recent authors include former Children's Laureate Michael Morpurgo, adventurer Bear Grylls and Nick Ward, author of the Charlie Small Journals.

Art Gallery
Send Bizzy your paintings and drawings and his favourite wins an art set including some fab Staedtler goodies.

Puzzle Time!
Could you find Eric? Unscramble Anna Gram's words? Tackle our hard puzzles? If so, winners receive fab prizes.

The Brainiacs
Scribbler!'s own gang of wiz kids are always on hand to help with spellings, alternative words and writing styles, they'll get you on the right track!

Prizes
Every issue we give away fantastic prizes. Recent prizes include Staedtler goodies, signed copies of Bear Grylls' books and posters, signed copies of Ricky Gervais' books, Charlie Small goodie bags, family tickets to The Eden Project, The Roald Dahl Museum & Story Centre and Alton Towers, a digital camera, books and writing sets galore and many other fab prizes!

... plus much more!
We keep you up to date with all the happenings in the world of literature, including blog updates from the Children's Laureate.

*If you are too old for Scribbler! magazine or have an older friend who enjoys creative writing, then check out Wordsmith. Wordsmith is for 11-18-year-olds and is jam-packed full of brilliant features, young writers' work, competitions and interviews too. For further information check out **www.youngwriters.co.uk** or ask an adult to call us on (01733) 890066.*

To get an adult to subscribe to either magazine for you, ask them to visit the website or give us a call.

Animal Riddle

As S wift as a swooping owl.
It attacks its P rey and traps it
With I ts glistening, soft
D ark cobweb.
It sucks fli E s' blood out all day long.
R eady to go to bed it makes its web.

Katie Hemmings (9)
Longlands Primary School & Nursery, Broxbourne

Untitled
(Inspired by Roald Dahl's 'Revolting Rhymes')

She is smaller than a chair leg
She is cute and cuddly
She is as noisy as a steam train
She is as quiet as a mouse
She is my baby sister.

Isaac Biggs (9)
Longtown Community Primary School, Longtown

Mot
(Inspired by Roald Dahl's 'Revolting Rhymes')

He is tragic
Instead of magic
He's quirky as a gadget
Fun on the trampoline
Where he likes to be seen.

Hannah Williams (9)
Longtown Community Primary School, Longtown

Llomy!
(Inspired by Roald Dahl's 'Revolting Rhymes')

She is as fast as a jet.
She is kind like a little mother hen.
She is as smiley as a ripe banana.
She is as dark as the sky at night.
It's my other self, Llomy!

Molly Watts (9)
Longtown Community Primary School, Longtown

Scarborough

S eagulls swooping in thin air
C rabs hiding in the rock pool
A rcades everywhere I go
R ock so very popular
B rand new DVDs being sold
O n top of the castle
R ock pool full with crabs
O pening the museum door
U nderwater crabs
G inormous beaches
H igh echoes in the sky.

Reyad West (9)
Lydgate Junior School, Sheffield

Gymnastics

As I walk through the door
I feel adored.

I sense my competition
There are thousands of people
Waiting for admission
My legs are shaking as I
Wait to fulfil my ultimate mission.

I'm excited but scared
I'm feeling sick
My tummy's going round
I've got butterflies.

I call my partner over
She says we're on soon
Giving me a reassuring smile.

We twist, flip, jump and skip
The crowd go *whoooo*
As we jump like kangaroos.

We both bow
The crowd
Goes *wow!*

Gymnastics is the best!

Liddy Lacey (11)
Magdalen Gates Primary School, Norwich

The Tiger

She pounces . . .
Up and down,
Up and down
And down and up,
Down and up.
She strikes like a lightning bolt
As her prey goes past.
She eats any animal that she can see.
She gobbles up very slowly,
So her prey will suffer pain
Just like her mother and father did.
As she runs in the forest,
She looks everywhere.
Nothing can defeat her,
She is too powerful
For anything or anyone.

Ashleigh Chester (10)
Magdalen Gates Primary School, Norwich

Age

I am getting to that age,
Where most things start to change.
The hair that's on my head is on my eyebrows instead.
My lines resemble lace,
I need to take an iron to my face.
My earlobes are hairy
And kids find me scary.
I'm down in the mouth as it's going south.
No more a teenager.
My clothes are getting bigger.
So here I lay and continue to decay.
At least I can be grateful, life is still eventful.

Laina Seaman (10)
Magdalen Gates Primary School, Norwich

Cats And Dogs

Cats and dogs always fight,
They always, always fight at night.
Dogs like noise, they like to play with their toys.
Cats are sneaky but very, very cheeky.
But they both like to play and fight all day.
Puppies are cool, they like to swim in the pool.
Kittens would look funny in mittens.
Cats like to climb trees but they don't like to get fleas.
Dogs like to play but they're unhappy when they don't get their own way.
Cats like stars.
Dogs like cars.
The only thing you can't stop them doing is fighting at night.

Madeleine Power (10)
Magdalen Gates Primary School, Norwich

Ogres, Trolls And Dragons

Ogres, trolls and dragons
Some are big, some are small,
Some are titchy, some are tall,
Some are smart, some are dumb,
Some are less talkative than your thumb,
Some are great,
Some are bait,
When they eat a banana they have a drama,
They're ogres, trolls and dragons.

Max Simpson (10)
Magdalen Gates Primary School, Norwich

Skateboarding

I love my skateboard,
It's fun to ride.
I love my skateboard,
To play outside.
I love my skateboard,
My wheels and trucks.
Without my skateboard life would suck.

Greg Waters (10)
Magdalen Gates Primary School, Norwich

Stars

The stars are shining in the night
Scattered in the sky so bright
I love the sight of sparkling light
It makes me feel delight
Tonight.

Hannah Donger (10)
Magdalen Gates Primary School, Norwich

I Know A Place In Africa

I know a place in Africa,
Where the white horses of the sea crash against the shore
And the silky sand slides between my toes,
Where the sun will burn my back at early dawn
And the cool breeze blows past my face.

I know a place in Africa,
Where I can taste the salty sea in the air
And the beautiful birds sing a song for Africa,
Where the never-ending vines of green climb up twigs and trees
And the twittering of children playing on the sand.

I know a place in Africa,
Where honeybees hover round their hives
And the gorgeous flowers reach for the sky,
Where I feel a butterfly tickling my nose
And the mysterious mountains ever upwards.

I know a place in Africa,
Where the moist, green grass tickles my toes
And the sun makes my back tingle like electricity,
Where the sunset eliminates the skies
And the mystical rain drips down my face.

I know a place in Africa,
Where fairy tales are told in caves
And the frosty sea covers the ocean,
Where the jewel of the sea twinkles in my eyes
And the lizards creep through the sand.

This is a place of cruelty and danger,
Where the bubble bursts and hope is released.

Leah King (10)
Molehill Copse Primary School, Maidstone

I Know A Place In Africa

I know a place in Africa
Where I can feel the warm breeze stroking my face
And the smooth sand slowly sinking me deeper
Where I can hear the voice of happiness brightening my day
And the waves making the sand soggy like dough.

I know a place in Africa
Where I can hear the mountains eating white candyfloss leaving a baby-blue sky
And the dark blue toucans spread while singing songs of joy and happiness
Where the hills make valleys of lush green grass
And the bushes of despair turn into a lighter green of hope.

I know a place in Africa
Where I can hear the crackling of lightning bolts thrown to Earth
And the drum of thunder
Where I can breathe the sadness and create joyful people
And taste the bitterness of despair and the sweetness of joy.

This is a place of freedom
Of explorers and tribal people
Where unlit country and light made the country free of living people
And miracles

This is a place of despair
Of sand dunes and trees of dead bodies
Where footways end and murderers track game
Of oblivion and showdowns
Where travels start and the sunsets look like fire.

Where brightness came and despair was obliterated.

Bradley Stolton (10)
Molehill Copse Primary School, Maidstone

I Know A Place In Africa

I know a place in Africa
Where I can feel the tranquil sand across my feet
And the scorching sun corrupts my back
Where I can hear the feathers of colourful birds
And the aromatic scent of saltwater fills the air

I know a place in Africa
Where the animals run wild and free
And the trees above shelter reams of colour below
Where the children's laughs echo through the city
And the fluorescence coats my vision

I know a place in Africa
Where I can hear the calls of the crimson birds
And watch their bodies afloat in the air
Where I can breathe the scent of falling mountains
And taste the caressing air through the jungle

This is a place of enigma
Of mystery and secrets
Where animals fall foul and Man brings them through
Of thoughts and memories beautiful

This is a place of distress
Of misery and sadness
Where tragedy pulls us low into the ground
Of catastrophe and hurt

Where paths end and mountains fall

Where hope burns through and angels sing songs of Africa.

Nathan Baker (10)
Molehill Copse Primary School, Maidstone

I Know A Place In Africa

I know a place in Africa
Where I can feel the warm, scorching sun rest on me
And the soft, tender sand goes between my feet
Where I can hear cheerful seagulls flying past happily
On the warm, gentle breeze

In a place in Africa
Where the white, bright sea crashes
And the beautiful city's in the gloomy night
Where the green emerald shines in the sun
And the bushes are full of fresh, luscious strawberries

In a place in Africa
Where I can hear the voice of religious gods
And watch their angels being sent to Earth
Where I can breathe sandy beaches and taste
The luscious scent of dewdrops

This is a place of freedom
Of freedom of joy
Where sombre looms and light is nowhere to be found
Of disgrace and memorials

This is a place of sadness and happiness
Of emerald forests and sapphire seas
Where poverty ends and changes lives
Of wonderful stuff and gloomy cities
Where journeys start and everything will be together once again.

BJ Okubule (10)
Molehill Copse Primary School, Maidstone

I Know A Place In Africa

I know a place in Africa
Where I can feel the sand tickling my toes gently
Where I can see the bright sun right in front of me
And where all the playful children are running about and screaming
As they step into the freezing cold water of the deep blue sea

I know a place in Africa
Where I can hear the zebras and lions fighting
As they charge into each other like a herd of rhinos
And I can see the pointy mountains touching the blue sky
And the white snow slowly falling to the ground

I know a place in Africa
Where the dull flowers turn bright in colour
And the butterflies delicately tickle my sensitive skin
As she flies around the beautiful trees
Where the trees are towering high above the clouds

I know a place in Africa
Where I can see the deep blue sea crashing up against the rough rocks
And where I can just sit on the sand, lay down and relax
And forget about all the sad things that have happened in life
And watch the beautiful gulls gracefully flying in the sapphire-blue sky

This is a place of freedom
Where hope is in every corner and happiness in every heart
And where our hearts are full of bliss and belief.

Rebeckah Kendall (10)
Molehill Copse Primary School, Maidstone

I Know A Place In Africa

I know a place in Africa
Where I can feel the sun kissing my face softly
And the sand rises between my toes
Where I can hear the happy sound of children playing on the shore

I know a place in Africa
Where the emerald-green of the jungle spreads like an eternal football
And lakes travel through like a blue snake
Where mountains and skyline struggle to dominate
And the turquoise wraps its comforting around the country

I know a place in Africa
Where I can hear the voice of the singing sunshine
And watch its beautiful rays launch over the desert
Where I can breathe the destruction of the desert
And taste its wrath

This is the place of freedom
Of depression and experience
Where darkness shattered and the light grew
Of living legends and miracles

This is a place of struggle
Of thorn trees and desert rats
Where the sand cooks like an oven
And its people cower from its power.

Aaron Biggs (10)
Molehill Copse Primary School, Maidstone

I Know A Place In Africa

I know a place in Africa
Where I can feel the summer's soft breeze calling my name
And the sand is soft like grain

I know a place in Africa
Where the mountains reach the sky
And the birds soar high above, whispering the songs of Africa

I know a place in Africa
Where I can hear the waves crash against the rugged rocks
And the baby-blue sky shines on the mountains
I can feel its warmth on my back

I know a place in Africa
Where the emerald jungle sleeps slowly
Where I can hear the turquoise river meandering by
And a waterfall, tall as a skyscraper, crashes down to meet its watery end

This is a place of struggle
Hope and sadness
No matter what it is
The people stand strong.

Scott Haxell (10)
Molehill Copse Primary School, Maidstone

I Know A Place In Africa

I know a place in Africa
Where I can feel the soft summer breeze calling my name
And the sand was tickling my toes till I surrendered to its message.

I know a place in Africa
Where peace and freedom lay on the floor in front of me
Violence should be overturned and peace takes its place.

I know a place in Africa
Where the jungle is a bright emerald
And hotels paint the skyline grey
Where the morning skies cry for freedom
And sunsets run like a river of blood.

I know a place in Africa where the mountains knock on the clouds
And heaven speaks to me.

Charlie Spice (10)
Molehill Copse Primary School, Maidstone

I Know A Place In Africa

I know a place in Africa
Where I can feel the warm sun on my back
Where I can hear the big waves crash on the great shore.

I know a place in Africa
Where I can see the red sun go down
Where the mountains touch the blue sky
And I feel the sand between my feet.

I know a place in Africa
Where I can hear cheerful children playing on the shore
Where I can feel deep blue water around my knees.

I know a place in Africa
Where I can hear the sound of screaming fans
As the World Cup goes on all the time.

I know a place in Africa
Where I can smell hot dogs from the hot dog stand
Where I can see men surfing on the big blue waves.

Ryan Moore (10)
Molehill Copse Primary School, Maidstone

I Know A Place In Africa

I know a place in Africa
Where I can feel the warm water
Soaking my toes,
I can hear the children playing
In the sand and in the water.

I know a place in Africa
Where the crabs pinch their claws
I can see the crabs dance the crab dance
From the sea to the shore.

I know a place in Africa
Where the sky is always blue
With fluffy candyfloss clouds spreading all over the sky
I can hear the little birds singing their little song.

I know a place in Africa
Where so many people die each day.

Ashleah Parsloe (10)
Molehill Copse Primary School, Maidstone

I Know A Place In Africa

I know a place in Africa
Where I can feel the sun tickling my toes
Where I can see the bright blue water right in front of me

I know a place in Africa
Where the sun is in the clouds
I can hear the birds above my head
I can feel a delicate butterfly on the tip of my nose

I know a place in Africa
Where I can see a ruby-red sky
Where a big ball of fire is falling down behind a silver, silky mountain
Touching the blue, cloudy sky

I know a place in Africa
Where the sun goes down and recedes
I can see the emerald-green trees
I am amazed at how many animals I can see everywhere

I know a place in Africa
Where the golden sun blazes onto the bright yellow sand
As I lay there
The grey seagulls fly over the white, soft clouds

Now the sun shines bright, brighter than ever.

Kayleigh Wood Davis (10)
Molehill Copse Primary School, Maidstone

I Know A Place In Africa

I know a place in Africa
Where I can feel the sand tickling my toes
Where I can see the bright blue water right in front of me.

I know a place in Africa
Where the sun is in the clouds
I can hear the birds above my head
I can feel the delicate butterfly on the tip of my nose.

I know a place in Africa
Where I can see a ruby-red sky
Where a big ball of fire falls down behind
A silver, silky mountain, touching the blue, cloudy sky.

I know a place in Africa
Where the sun goes down and recedes
I can see the emerald trees, I am amazed at
How many animals I see everywhere.

I know a place in Africa
Where the golden sun blazes onto the bright yellow sand
As I lie there in peace
The grey seagulls fly over the white, soft clouds.

Rose Tucker (10)
Molehill Copse Primary School, Maidstone

I Know A Place In Africa

I know a place in Africa
Where I can see the light of the sunshine
And feel it on my back,
The waves crashing against the tall but steady rocks
On the endless golden shore.

I know a place in Africa
Where the mountains touch the sky
Of sapphire-blue (but do not erupt)
The trees in which the birds sleep.

I know a place in Africa
Where I can hear the thunder gods
Whispering and shouting out loud,
The rain clouds raining with laughter and crying as well.

This is a place of happiness
To be free and have peace
To walk around a street
Prancing about.

Avalon Monk (10)
Molehill Copse Primary School, Maidstone

Dragons

Dragons are a strange lot
No two are quite the same.
Some like to scale tall mountains.
Some don't even have a name.
Some have horns and teeth and wings.
Some just like to sit.
Some love to go out flying.
Some love to rage and spit.

So if you've seen a dragon,
Consider yourself blessed,
Because of all the creatures in the world,
He's picked you out as best.
And if he follows you around,
Decides to take you home,
Know ye well that he will be
A friend you truly own.

Zachary Mason (9)
Prenton Prep School, Prenton

I Saw A Dragon

You may not believe me,
But I saw something way up high in the sky,
I saw a dragon flying up so very high.

Swooping over the glades,
Wings like blades.
Soaring through the sky
Like a bullet with a red, fiery eye.

Feet the size of boulders came crashing to the ground,
The earth started to shake with a tremendous sound.

Teeth like swords,
Talons of steel,
Breath of fire,
Enough to make you reel.
Scales ice-blue,
Like a living statue.

I saw a dragon,
Maybe one day you will too!

Samuel Cross (9)
Prenton Prep School, Prenton

My Pet Dragon

My pet dragon is called Tim
He is so small he could fit in a bin.

He is very vicious and scary
But the only food he eats is dairy!

In the morning Tim eats cheese
Too much makes him sneeze!

In the evening he has his teddy Ted
Then he drifts off to bed.

Hannah Das (9)
Prenton Prep School, Prenton

Dragon's Tale

Hello, my name is Stanley,
And we dragons are tough and manly.
We have big, bulging eyes,
And our favourite food is pies,
Made from meat that is humanly!

Now when you come and fight,
Watch out because we bite!
Beware our fire is hot
And *will* burn you on the bot
As you run from me, what a sight!

But when our little ones are young,
They track you with their tongue!
Their cries are shrill,
When they catch you, what a thrill
For you become a steaming pile of dung!

Christopher Hall (9)
Prenton Prep School, Prenton

The Dragon In My Garden

The dragon in my garden is very, very shy,
Once I managed to see him fly.
When I first saw him I thought he was fierce,
With his huge jaws designed to pierce.
I've tried feeding him all sorts of things,
All he'll eat is fried chicken wings.

The dragon in my garden is covered in blue scales,
His feet are so huge that he squashes the snails!
At night-time he prowls,
Spying on the owls,
But he's not so shy anymore,
I can tickle his belly and he rolls on the floor!

Tom Johnson (9)
Prenton Prep School, Prenton

Dragon Horror

I am a dragon.
I have a horrible mouth
And I make you eat trout.
I am a big liar
And I breathe fire.
My name is Tame
And I'll give you a nasty pain.
Never fight with me
Or you will end up weak.

Heather Davies (9)
Prenton Prep School, Prenton

Love

Love is a strawberry.
It tastes like sweets.
Love smells like flowers.
It looks like a heart.
Love sounds like a crumbling noise.
It feels like playing.
Love reminds me of Eid.

Zainab Uddin (8)
Quwwat-ul-Islam Girls' School, Forest Gate

Love

Love is red like hearts,
It tastes like sweets.
Love smells like a delicious curry,
It looks like people hugging.
Love sounds like joyful laughter,
It feels like comfort.
It reminds me of Heaven.

Aamena Bhikhi (9)
Quwwat-ul-Islam Girls' School, Forest Gate

Love

Love is pink like small hearts.
Love tastes like sweet bubblegum.
Love smells like pink strawberry cake.
Love looks like twinkling stars.
Love sounds like joyful Eid.
It feels like hugs and kisses.
It reminds me of weddings.

Sheikh Jubaydah Mariam Rahman (9)
Quwwat-ul-Islam Girls' School, Forest Gate

Happiness

Happiness is pink like the morning sun,
It tastes like candyfloss twirling in my mouth,
Happiness smells like an orange daffodil,
It looks like a sparkling star.
Happiness sounds like laughing children,
It feels like a jump of joy.
Happiness reminds me of my first best friend!

Ameera Vawda (8)
Quwwat-ul-Islam Girls' School, Forest Gate

Love

Love is red like strawberries.
It tastes like strawberry jam.
Love smells like pink blossom.
It looks like love hearts.
Love sounds like a drum.
It feels like playing with my friends.
Love reminds me of Eid.

Asmaa Uddin (8)
Quwwat-ul-Islam Girls' School, Forest Gate

Plants And Animals

The flower grows tall,
The seeds stay small.

The grass is long,
The birds sing a song.

The bees make honey,
We buy it for money.

Ladybirds crawl!
Birds call.

Chickens lay eggs,
They have two legs.

Children play on the ground,
They make a big sound.

Charlotte Yorke (7)
Roberts Primary School, Dudley

The Brawl

In the brawl of 50 that takes 100 tries
Died has many and lost so many lives.
Blood has been shed, bright and blood-red,
It has leaked on the hard stone floor.
Creatures cried out, were thrown about
And landed in a painful heap.
At last the prize has been won,
Like fire in darkness, the victors light up the night
With the happiness in their souls,
But the brawl is never finished.

Cameron Kelly (10)
St Faith's CE Primary School, Norwich

Football Match

At the kick-off
The stadium is full
They're about to kick-off
When, oh no, a flat ball!
Two minutes from kick-off
A penalty against
It couldn't get any worse
They just have to hope it's a save!

The penalty is taken
The keeper tries to put him off
He succeeds in doing it
He blasts it over the bar!

25 minutes gone
The score is still 0-0
The midfield has put the striker in
And at last, a goal to us!

At half-time
The score is 1-0
They know that they are the better side
The possession is 53:47.

50 minutes in
The score is 1-0
When the defender slides in
He has got to go!

It's a free kick to us
They're going to try a trick
Two players dummy it
And the third smashes it in.

The keeper's hand has broken
The shot was just so hard
The sub-keeper comes on
The score is 2-0.

5 minutes stoppage time
They're up the other end
The opponents' striker's been put in
And the final score's 2-1.

James Pye (9)
St Faith's CE Primary School, Norwich

World War II

Soldiers are fighting deep, deep in the trenches
Fighting, wounding, killing, dying
Although there is death, murder and horrible stenches
The soldiers keep fighting for their country

Tanks are charging big and strong
Firing huge, ginormous shells
Teams try to take them out, be careful not to do anything wrong
As the tanks go on and on

Spitfires fight high in the sky
Firing their deadly rounds
Brave young pilots prepared to die
To stop the enemy bombs

People in the submarines following their lines
On long distance missions
Using stealth to dodge the mines
And inside they run like rats so everything is good

And that is how the war was won
Fighting to the bloody end
Never ever stopping until all is good and done.

Samuel Manning (10)
St Faith's CE Primary School, Norwich

Snow

One snowy day the snow whistled and whispered
Amongst the starry night.
The snowflakes whistled around and around
Like a whirlwind.
All the snowmen had carrots for noses, stones for buttons
And sticks for arms.
The children wrapped up warm with hat, gloves, scarf
And welly boots.
Hearing the boots crunch along the snow
Is like someone eating a chocolate biscuit.
Full moon ahead, cats prepare to snuggle up warm
In front of the flickering fire.
All you can see out of the windows
Are bare trees and snow.

Megan Howe (10)
St Faith's CE Primary School, Norwich

The Wonders Of Autumn

As the wind gently whispers,
Conkers fall from the trees,
Softly landing on beds of leaves
That some weeks ago
Landed on the unset ground.
They fall so quietly, without a sound.

A little boy picks up the conkers,
He laughs at the way they're cold and smooth.
He sees the other conkers all spiky and green,
Only his prize conker is shiny and brown
And the conker remembers what he used to be
When he gently fell on a bed of leaves
That crunched like a bag of crisps.

Eleanor Garner (10)
St Faith's CE Primary School, Norwich

The Trenches

Tanks are rumbling,
The floor is crumbling,
The guns are firing,
Planes are falling,
The trenches small bad,
Bombs are flying to Earth,
The guns are heavy,
My socks are smelly,
People are flying,
Then they're dying,
Tanks are turning to ash,
So please just shut the door,
So please just stop this horrid war.

Peter Savory (9)
St Faith's CE Primary School, Norwich

Dogz

Daschunds are long, greyhounds are thin,
Bulldogs are fat and Chihuahuas are slim.

Huskies like to rock and spaniels like to hip hop,
Akitas like to sing, Great Danes like to dance.

Jack Russells like to rap,
Some poodles like to sing really, really high
And Shiatsus like to dance.

German Shepherds like to play I-Spy
And sheepdogs like to play mud pies!

Dalmatians like to play chess
And Labradors like to make a big *mess!*

Shakira Clifton (11)
St Faith's CE Primary School, Norwich

War Zone

I can hear the guns clattering and clashing,
The big missiles screeching past my ear,
The scruffy men came to, when planes
Brought missiles dropping over our heads.

When I'm in the trenches it crackles and crumbles
On the floor, with men beside me who are
Fighting this war. When I look up in the sky,
I worry the plane will die.

The men lying in the mud
Is like a sausage in the middle
Of a puddle of gravy.

Callum Mel Flack (10)
St Faith's CE Primary School, Norwich

Autumn

A is for autumn, a lovely time of year
U is for umbrella, which you hold up with your dear
T is for trees that make conkers fall to the ground
U is for unusual for the things you have found
M is for marching through the woods, having a little mime
N is for nights that get darker and darker every time.

Charlotte Dack (10)
St Faith's CE Primary School, Norwich

Autumn Winds

Autumn winds blowing leaves off the trees,
Conkers falling like it's raining big brown peas,
Leaves falling in big coloured crowds,
Red, yellow and orange in the wind which howls.
Pine cones, hazelnuts on the ground,
Crunch, crunch, under our shoes.
Little children fighting over conkers, whose is whose?
Squirrels squeaking, climbing up trees,
Dropping nuts as they climb.
Holding up your umbrella in the autumn rain,
Can't wait for summer, everyone groans!

Chloe Edwards (9)
St Faith's CE Primary School, Norwich

Kangaroo

Where did he come from?
Where did he go?
Kangaroo, you fool,
Where did he come from?
Where did he go?
King kangaroo.
Kangaroo bounded around the gusty plains,
Like a slithering snake.
Where do you go
King kangaroo?

Ben Lockwood (9)
St Faith's CE Primary School, Norwich

World At War

Tanks are rumbling,
The floor is crumbling,
The guns are firing,
A plane gets shot down.
The trenches smell bad,
My food fell from the sky.
The guns are heavy,
My feet are smelly
And bombs fall from the sky.

Jack Willey (10)
St Faith's CE Primary School, Norwich

Cats

Cats run like a racing car
Cats are cute
Cats curl up on Mum's best chair
Cats go miaow, miaow, miaow
Cats are fast
Cats chase rabbits
Cats play with you, you, you
Cats are sweet
Like a chocolate cake.

Esme Barham-Brown (9)
St Faith's CE Primary School, Norwich

Autumn Nights

One autumn night leaves on the trees crackle and crunch,
The squirrels scatter on the walls and trees,
Trying to find nuts for their huts.
The conkers fall while we snore,
The poor old hedgehogs scatter through the night.
The sticks are like long pencils breaking,
While the twigs are snapping like pieces of paper ripping.

Bethany Mannall (10)
St Faith's CE Primary School, Norwich

Swimming

Swimming, sliding, sweating, in the swimming pool,
Riding on the slide, in the swimming pool,
Sitting in the bubbles, in the swimming pool,
Diving underwater, in the swimming pool,
Jumping in the water, in the swimming pool
The sound of my body crashing is like a bomb going *boom!*

Bailey Chapman (10)
St Faith's CE Primary School, Norwich

Autumn's Here

A is for acorns falling from the trees
U is for unusual plants, perfect for the bees
T is for toads jumping from the pond side
U is for underground where lots of animals hide
M is for morning, lovely at this time of year
N is for November, autumn's finally here!

Charlotte Raywood (10)
St Faith's CE Primary School, Norwich

My Cat

Noisy miaower
Fast eater
Silly friend
Racing chasing
High jumper
Always play
Any day
Lazy always
Good cats
Are fun!

Melissa Neish (9)
St Joseph's RC School, Aberdeen

History

H istory is fun
I like drawing about history
S ee this book for history, read it
T o people who like history, read it
O kay, let's say it is a magical book
R ead the book, it is the best
Y ou will enjoy it.

Deborah Fatogun (8)
St Joseph's RC School, Aberdeen

Divers

D ivers are black and red
I nky black suits and that
V arious divers are everywhere
E veryone sees them in aquariums
R ed divers are great
S ea creatures see them all the time.

Fraser Lambert (9)
St Joseph's RC School, Aberdeen

Love

L ove is like happiness
O ut loud
V iolet colour of love
E ndless love.

Hannah Ellington (9)
St Joseph's RC School, Aberdeen

Love

Love feels warm, soft, glowing and flowing,
Love tastes like candy and moves like a gentle wind,
Love smells like flowers early in the morning,
Love is like crunching leaves twisting and tumbling all around,
Love is a bright red sun.

Michael O'Brien (9)
St Malachy's Primary School, Newry

119

I Will Put In My Box . . .
(Inspired by 'Magic Box' by Kit Wright)

I will put in the box . . .

The fire of dragons' breath toasting 100,000 marshmallows.
A chocolate bar dancing to the cha-cha slide.
Ashley and Jones running with the mascots.

I will put in the box . . .

The first step of my baby brother, Josh, he is as jumpy as a tiger.
The spikes on his head,
The splash of the milk from his bottle.

I will put in the box . . .

Cherry Cola fizzing like Fanta.
A dog's ears flapping up and down.
A Catherine wheel whizzing in the moonlight.

I will put in the box . . .

The loop on G-force.
The splash of the lovely log flume.
The splash of the rapids.

My box is fashioned from . . .

The touch of blue silk to the feel of the leopard's spots
And sapphires from the darkest cave.

Charlotte Harrison (8)
St Michael's CE (A) First School, Stafford

Magic Box
(Inspired by 'Magic Box' by Kit Wright)

I will put in the box . . .

A shining star shining,
Sparkling in the moonlight.
A gold, glittering, beautiful, astonishing bracelet
That the Queen wears on her wrist.
A laughing hyena giggling and having fun.

Saffron Jackson (8)
St Michael's CE (A) First School, Stafford

I Will Put In My Box . . .

(Inspired by 'Magic Box' by Kit Wright)

I will put in my box . . .

A unicorn's horn swirling round and round.
The Queen's first grape seed
As she is taking the seed elegantly.
A pencil as colourful as the rainbow.

I will put in my box . . .

The mascots running around.
The sun shining in the sky
As brightly as it can.
The sparkle and spike of a star.

I will put in my box . . .

The mascots starting in the Olympics.
A killer whale's squirt.
The artists masterpiece, like Picasso.

I will put in my box . . .

The Queen's favourite jewel.
The loudest snore of a giant.
The thinnest lead made from
The most colourful pieces of the rainbow.

My box is fashioned from . . .

The rainbow, with fish scales on the lid
And the tooth of a walrus.

Ellie Shirley (8)
St Michael's CE (A) First School, Stafford

The Magic Box
(Inspired by 'Magic Box' by Kit Wright)

I will put in the box . . .

Really tasty sweets that dance in your tummy.

I will put in the box . . .

Cherry Coke that plays about the mouth,
Turning your tongue luminous red.

I will put in the box . . .

Some sparkles glistening like blue water.
It sparkles like a DJ's disco ball.

The box is square and it is made of rainbow dust.

Daniel Lyons (8)
St Michael's CE (A) First School, Stafford

My Shiny Box
(Inspired by 'Magic Box' by Kit Wright)

I will put in the box . . .

Sparkling water flowing backwards.
The first walk of my baby cousin
And the cat exploring on its first night.

I will put in the box . . .

The first sound of a baby boy's chuckle.
The bouncing jelly jumping up and down
And the sky that's blue.

I will put in the box . . .

A boy and girl making friends.
A laptop finding stuff
And a gold night.

My box is fashioned from . . .

Red, shiny stickers,
Hearts like the shimmering sky
And loads of friendship.

Lucy Turley-Walker (8)
St Michael's CE (A) First School, Stafford

Magic Box

(Inspired by 'Magic Box' by Kit Wright)

I will put in the box . . .

The shining of an African sunbeam.
A banana dancing in the summer breeze.
The waves of Wales' beach.

I will put in the box . . .

Monkeys giggling all through the year.
Ten jelly beans all different flavours.
Eighteen candy canes as yummy as the Queen's cake.

My box is fashioned from . . .

Coconut bars from the freshest coconuts.
The handle is five Olympic medals, bronze, silver and gold.
It's decorated with fire wallpaper.

Oliver Jones (8)
St Michael's CE (A) First School, Stafford

My Box

(Inspired by 'Magic Box' by Kit Wright)

I will put in my box . . .

The skill of the wolves,
The brightness of the sun,
The stretchiest spaghetti.

I will put in my box . . .

Long, hairy kangaroo legs,
A crawling woodlouse looking for darkness,
A shimmering diamond like a star.

My box is fashioned from . . .

Burning hot lava like being in an oven,
Tiger footprints all over it,
A wolf's eye looking out at you.

Benjamin Wall (8)
St Michael's CE (A) First School, Stafford

Magic Box
(Inspired by 'Magic Box' by Kit Wright)

I will put in the box . . .

A goal of a legend
To save a penalty kick
To skill a legend.

I will put in the box . . .

A brittle bone of a dinosaur
A million-year-old bone
A really long footprint.

I will put in the box . . .

Michael Jackson dancing like a star
Him singing at a concert
Audience cheering.

My box is fashioned from . . .

Bright yellow gold
Glistening diamonds and
Red metal.

Liam Smith (8)
St Michael's CE (A) First School, Stafford

I Will Put In My Box . . .
(Inspired by 'Magic Box' by Kit Wright)

I will put in my box . . .

The bright light of the yellow sun,
The sourness of the juicy lemon,
The shine of the moonlight.

I will put in my box . . .

The bright sun dancing in the sky,
The beautiful, white, shining moonlight glowing on the moon,
The sparkling gold that shines like a diamond.

My box is fashioned from
Wood, metal and steel as hard as a rock.
The box is as brown as a bear.

Jessica-Marie Woods (8)
St Michael's CE (A) First School, Stafford

The Magic Box

(Inspired by 'Magic Box' by Kit Wright)

I will put in the box . . .

The splash of storm force 10 splashing at everyone,
A warm snowman dying to get in a freezer,
A sunflower smile as it dances in the wind.

I will put in the box . . .

All the colours of the rainbow shining in the sky,
A tail of a rabbit that has just come out of its mother,
A wave of a new baby's hand.

I will put in the box . . .

A newly built park as massive as a giant's big bath,
A trunk of an elephant as it jiggles when it has a cold,
The feel of G-force going slowly round.

My box is fashioned from . . .

Pink strips on the sides
With red and purple diamonds on the top.

Aimee Hawkins (8)
St Michael's CE (A) First School, Stafford

The Magic Box

(Inspired by 'Magic Box' by Kit Wright)

I will put in the box . . .

A glass, glistening pen,
So fragile that you can see right through it.
A rabbit's tail as fluffy and furry as cotton wool.
A meatball swimming backwards like a champion.

I will put in the box . . .

The skill of Wolverhampton Wanderers.
The five Olympic rings.

My box is fashioned from . . .

Sheep's coats as soft as a feather.
Leather as rough as a tree.
Ten bricks as hard as metal.

Callum Morgan (8)
St Michael's CE (A) First School, Stafford

Magic Box
(Inspired by 'Magic Box' by Kit Wright)

I will put in the box . . .

An aeroplane's wing
Curved like a clock face.

I will put in the box . . .

A train's wheel
Spinning like the sun.

I will put in the box . . .

A duck's beak
As sharp as a shark's tooth.

I will put in the box . . .

All the colours of the rainbow
Like the glass of a window.

My box is fashioned from
Gold, iron and red diamonds.

Jordan Ryan (8)
St Michael's CE (A) First School, Stafford

Magic Box
(Inspired by 'Magic Box' by Kit Wright)

I will put in the box . . .

Glowing, shining sea, tipping it slowly
To stop it getting away.

I will put in the box . . .

A big can of Coke,
It is cold and brown.

I will put in the box . . .

A bright sun and it comes every day,
It sparkles like a lamp.

Daniel Bridgwood (9)
St Michael's CE (A) First School, Stafford

My Magic Box
(Inspired by 'Magic Box' by Kit Wright)

I will put in my box . . .

A flame of a dragon's burning breath
As hot as an oven.
A piece of silk from a spider's web.
A load of colourful pencils as pretty as a rainbow.

I will put in the box . . .

A drop of rain floating down from the misty air.
The two mascots running in the Olympics.
A sip of Coca-Cola fizzing in your mouth.

I will put in the box . . .

The first flicker of the stars in the dark night.

My box is fashioned from . . .

A piece of ribbon as red as roses.
Sparkling card and lots of paints as bright as safety jackets.

Hannah Birch (8)
St Michael's CE (A) First School, Stafford

I Will Put In The Box . . .
(Inspired by 'Magic Box' by Kit Wright)

I will put in the box . . .

Big beefy burgers
Scrumptious and lovely.

I will put in the box . . .

Creamy melted chocolate made of cocoa
Smells like a cup of hot chocolate.

I will put in the box . . .

A strong gold chain with a blue stone
Swinging like a monkey.

Brandon Sheldon (9)
St Michael's CE (A) First School, Stafford

The Mystery Magic Box
(Inspired by 'Magic Box' by Kit Wright)

I will put in the box . . .

My German Shepherd's two moles
That are as his ears are down.

A tiger with a huge paw banging the ground
As it stalks its prey.

A pig's swirly tail as it swirls and spins
In the funny wind.

I will put in the box . . .

The longest piece of spaghetti,
As long as St Michael's school building.

A huge bees' nest with lots of honey in it,
The honey is as lovely as a rose's scent.

The sun's wind in the freezing North Pole,
That is as lovely as a newborn baby.

Mya Bagria (8)
St Michael's CE (A) First School, Stafford

I Will Put In My Box . . .
(Inspired by 'Magic Box' by Kit Wright)

I will put in my box . . .

A leprechaun's gold
As they stand at the end of the rainbow.
The Statue of Liberty singing and dancing.
A very large book being read by a king.

I will put in my box . . .

Every car's dirty, smelly number plate.
The embarrassing sweat of a man while he waits.

I will put in my box . . .

A pyramid made by Egyptians millions of years ago.
A shadow of a snail as it moves slowly.

Millie-Rose Price (9)
St Michael's CE (A) First School, Stafford

Imagination

As I sit here watching the sky,
I see lots of creatures floating by.

Witches and wizards,
With crooked old wands,
Fishes and mermaids
Diving in ponds.

Fire-breathing dragons,
With rusty red wings,
Burning down houses
And trampling on kings.

Fantasy creatures,
As strange as can be,
Open your eyes
And then you will see . . .

Neha Morrison (10)
St Monica's RC Primary School, Appleton

Environment

E veryone should throw litter in the bin
N obody should do a silly sin
V andalism is bad
I t makes people sad
R ace to make the world bright
O n the cliffs to see a stunning sight
N othing should make you drop litter
M y mum said litter is bitter
E verywhere is not so clean
N aughty people are being mean
T hink about the planet, don't throw litter on the floor!

That is all I have to say, not much more!

Charlie Brandwood (10)
St Monica's RC Primary School, Appleton

129

Roller Coaster Ride

Have you been on roller coasters?
Look on amusement park posters.
I'm telling you so you know,
So you're ready for when we go.

Cos when you sit in the chair,
You don't have a care.
Until the key turns,
And to your concern,
It starts . . .

Twirling and whirling,
And curling and hurling.
Going furiously fast,
Everything's whizzing past.

Then you're at the top,
There's a long vertical drop.
Then you get a feeling in your tummy,
The carriage moves and you call for Mummy.

You feel the track quake,
You're sure it's going to break.
You can smell terror and fear,
Because we're . . .
On a roller coaster ride!

So I advise you,
And I know it's true,
Stay away from roller coasters
And amusement park posters.

If you can't stand . . .

Twirling and whirling,
And curling and hurling,
Going furiously fast,
Everything's whizzing past

Because it's . . .
A roller coaster ride!

Maegan Spiteri (10)
St Monica's RC Primary School, Appleton

Nature's Greatest Desire

The sun shone brightly,
Sweetly, full with excitement,
The birds sang with exuberance,
The sky twinkled with life,
Surrounded by bright, puffy clouds
Which looked like cotton candy floating in thin air.
Trees waving their branches about,
Here and there,
The wind rushing its way past the nature
And whistling its mystical tunes,
Gliding and slicing past
The illuminated green grass.

Sarah Rodrigues (11)
St Monica's RC Primary School, Appleton

Holiday Fevers

The aeroplane went as high as a kite,
When I got there I was sure the birds would bite.
All of the sand,
Feels soft in your hand,
The crisp blue sea runs smoothly,
Just like me.
All my family were there,
Giving me all the love and care,
But I was glad that,
I had a fabulous *holiday!*

Morgan Unsworth (10)
St Monica's RC Primary School, Appleton

Summer And Winter

Summer and winter can change your life, do you know?
How many times couldn't you go outside because of the rain or snow?
Summer can be a blast, people everywhere,
We play in parks, football, climbing trees, eating ice cream
And that is only the beginning.
Wintertime, snowballs thrown, sledges pushed, snow angels made.
What a fabulous time you can have.
Do you think we're lucky to have these seasons?

Marcus Sinclair (10)
St Monica's RC Primary School, Appleton

Penguins

A penguin I am and what a fabulous model!
You can watch me dance around, *waddle, waddle, waddle!*

I'm jumping, I'm skipping, I'm a bird that cannot fly,
I'm sliding, I'm hopping and I'm never ever shy.

Watch me hit the water as I leap and dive in,
The sea is my home and I swim around in a spin.

I hunt for fish daily, for my lunch and dinner,
I love snow and ice and cold weather, what a winner!

Come, come and see me here in the frozen north,
With hats, scarves, gloves and a coat, of course!

Gerry Bryant (9)
St Nicholas CE Primary School, Shepperton

Butter On The Plate

Butter on the plate
Butter on the plate
Slip, slide, slip, slide
Butter on the plate.

Fish on the hook
Fish on the hook
Wiggle, waggle, wiggle, waggle
Fish on the hook.

Dog in the pond
Dog in the pond
Splish, splash, splish, splash
Dog in the pond.

Bee on the flower
Bee on the flower
Bizz, buzz, bizz, buzz
Bee on the flower.

Bird in the air
Bird in the air
Flip, flap, flip, flap
Bird in the air.

Soup in my bowl
Soup in my bowl
Slop!

Emily French (9)
St Nicholas CE Primary School, Shepperton

Football, Football, Football

Football, football, football,
Better than school,
Football, football, football,
Fun for all,
Sunday is my day,
For my team plays,
Dash to the ball,
Always first,
But if last,
Tackle hard,
Make sure,
No red card,
Scoring goal,
The crowd cheers,
Game's at an end,
So it's time for ginger beer!

William Wells (9)
St Nicholas CE Primary School, Shepperton

My Riverside Poem

Standing by the riverside,
A hare jumps out then runs to hide.

In the softly dappled light,
Ducks and geese take sudden flight.

Church bells ringing far away,
In the trees young squirrels play.

I tracked a heron passing by,
Majestically it swoops up high.

A wooden yacht glides silently by,
Its rainbow sail fluttering up high.

I left the river running there,
Its joys remain for all to share.

Louis Huang-Dixon (9)
St Nicholas CE Primary School, Shepperton

Transport

White
Blue
Silver
Grey
Where are they travelling today?
Lorry
Van
Car
Bus
I wonder if anyone's visiting us?
Black
Red
Yellow
Green
Where are they going?
Where have they been?
Cycle
Jog
Walk
Run
Better for me and much more fun!

Sara Garcia (9)
St Nicholas CE Primary School, Shepperton

Football

I'm a football nice and clean
When I am put on the green.

When I'm kicked I spin round
Sometimes high or on the ground.

When I hit the hard goalpost
That is when it hurts the most.

But when into the goal I go
The people cheer and then I know
I have made a cheerful crowd
That is when I feel proud.

Ethan Howick (9)
St Nicholas CE Primary School, Shepperton

Up For The Cup

It's Sunday morning, football time
And I'm racing down to breakfast,
Then rushing to get dressed,
Kit on, ready to go,
Mum shouts, 'Don't forget your shinpads and boots!'
Into the car with Dad, racing to the match,
'It's the cup final today!'
Meet with the team,
Everyone's excited and raring to go,
We line up and the ref blows the whistle,
Game on!
At the kick-off, the opposition steal the ball
And break towards our goal,
'Oh no! They've scored!'
Half-time and we're 1-0 down,
Grab our drinks and it's time for the team talk,
Second half and I get the ball,
Do a quick 1-2 and we've equalised, 1-1!
They kick-off and Charlie is through . . .
2-1!
Desperate for the ref to finish the game . . .
It's all over and we've won!
Hooray for the Colts!

Matthew Allen (10)
St Nicholas CE Primary School, Shepperton

Joe Plays Rugby

J oe played rugby on a hot summer's day
O ver the hills they went to play a rugby game
E nd of season, a tasty sausage on the BBQ.

Joseph Graves (9)
St Nicholas CE Primary School, Shepperton

Bunny World

My name is Lizzy,
I am truly frizzy,
I have a brother,
His name is Darcy,
He likes to party,
We live in a three-floored house,
We sometimes see a mouse,
His name is Lee
And he climbs our tree,
To see his family,
We love our carrots and broccoli,
It makes us grow immediately,
We like to wash now and then,
Counting from one to ten,
Now our story is over and done,
Do come again, it's number one!

Elise Parker (9)
St Nicholas CE Primary School, Shepperton

My Amazing Cat, Daisy

Daisy is my best friend
Although she is a cat
She never eats too much
But she is rather fat
She sleeps all day
And she sleeps all night
When she jumps on my bed
It can give me a fright
She miaows every day to get some attention
Now it is time for me to mention
Lucky for me
I have a cat
That is rather fat
The only thing she likes the most
Is me!
Because I love cats!
She is my best cat
And she is the fattest cat I know
And that's great for me!

Rowena White (9)
St Nicholas CE Primary School, Shepperton

The Magic Pie

There was a young boy called Kye,
Who ate a magic pie,
He found it on the floor
And he wasn't really sure,
That he should eat the pie,
Since it made him fly.

He zoomed up to the sky,
With the help of his magic pie,
When he reached the sun,
He realised what he'd done.
He'd gone up way too high
And now he started to fry.

He exclaimed out with a cry,
'I don't think I want to fly!'
He floated to the ground
And landed without a sound.
He turned his head and said goodbye,
Then he threw away his magic pie.

Sam Keene (9)
St Nicholas CE Primary School, Shepperton

My Rescue Cat

No animal is half as cute
As Maggie in her birthday suit
She's black and white
She's such a fright
She rolls in dirt all day and night.

She doesn't care about a thing
All she does is sleep in
And when the sun comes out to play
And all the rain has gone away
She brushes her hair and parties away.

She's so mischievous, my little cat
She crawls under gates and scratches the mat
She races up the garden path with me
I love my rescue cat from Battersea
Luckily she didn't come from Tennessee!

Emily Cullen (9)
St Nicholas CE Primary School, Shepperton

My White Rabbit

My rabbit's eyes are as blue as the gleaming sky
My rabbit's fur is as soft as a comforting pillow
My rabbit's whiskers are as thin as a pencil tip
My rabbit's paws are as wet as a human's tongue
My rabbit is as white as snow.

My rabbit eats as fast as he runs
My rabbit's teeth are as sharp as a shark's tooth
My rabbit's back legs are as strong as sofa legs
My rabbit gets cross and he thumps and thumps and thumps
My rabbit's tail is as short as a tree stump.

My rabbit's claws are as sharp as a razor
My rabbit's hutch is as grand as a castle
My rabbit's nose is as small as a button
My rabbit's name is Radcliffe Brooker
My love for my rabbit is bigger than the world.

Lauren Brooker (9)
St Nicholas CE Primary School, Shepperton

Football

I love playing football
I play it all the time
I'm really good at skills
And kick it very high.

I love playing forward
I play there all the time
I'm very good at shooting
And shoot it very high.

I love scoring goals
I've scored 22 times
I'm very good at accuracy
And that probably why

I can't wait to play again
. . . That reminds me, goodbye.

Tyler Newman (9)
St Nicholas CE Primary School, Shepperton

My Sister Loves Ballet!

My sister is called Jade
But I call her Jadey
And all her friends call her Spadey!
She dances everywhere
And has ribbons in her hair.
She jumps about like a cheerful sprout
And she jumps high
Like she can fly.
She is in a boarding school called Elmhurst
And it is in association with Birmingham Royal Ballet.
I think she is the best
When she dances with the rest!
This is my sister, champion Jade,
Jade's born with this talent specially made.

Ava Gibson (9)
St Nicholas CE Primary School, Shepperton

The Bogeyman

In the rainforest there lives a terrible creature
He lurks in the night with sharp piercing spikes
Sticking out of his back
He has long green fingernails
And massive hands to strangle people

Every night people see this horrible creature and run away
But the bogeyman is too fast
It drips with doom
When it's had its prey
And a crash of lightning always strikes down

Don't go near him
You should fear him
What will you do when he gets you?

Theo Knott (9)
St Nicholas CE Primary School, Shepperton

Our Pets

We have lots of pets in our family,
We have Milly, the dog, and Sparky, the green finch,
We have Lucky, the Bantam chick,
And five Chinese painted quail, whose names are too many to mention,
We have tropical fish,
One that's called Lucky,
Because he survived being stuck in the filter
And the goldfish and ghost carp who live in the pond,
Oh, don't forget the pet spiders too,
Do you know?
Sometimes I think I live in a zoo!

Ben Long (10)
St Nicholas CE Primary School, Shepperton

Space

Looking up at the sky
I wonder how high
I wonder how far
I wonder how long
It would take to reach a star?

Jupiter, Mars, Pluto and the sun
Are planets which make space fun

Wish I could fly to the moon
Just before the time was noon!

Keanu Swart (9)
St Nicholas CE Primary School, Shepperton

Race Day

Running races may be hard
But you just need to do your best
Run your fastest
Never stop
Then you will succeed

R un, run, never stop
A lways try your best
C atch them, catch them, catch them now
E verybody cheers, hooray!

Georgina Cosgrove (9)
St Nicholas CE Primary School, Shepperton

Tina Turner

Tina Turner likes sausages,
Tina Turner likes oranges,
Tina Turner plays all day,
Tina Turner sits around to sometimes eat all day,
Tina Turner goes to school,
Tina Turner breaks the rules,
Tina Turner is fast asleep,
Night-night Tina Turner,
You have to do it all over again tomorrow!

Chris Taylor (9)
St Nicholas CE Primary School, Shepperton

Animals

A ntelopes galloping along
N ever go near a lion
I guanas creeping through the rainforest
M ice squeaking quietly
A lligators hunting for zebra
L ively and fierce
S oft and cuddly
   No matter what they are
   I love them all the same.

Julia Tait (9)
St Nicholas CE Primary School, Shepperton

The River

Oh, the river, the river indeed
It will always succeed to please.

The beauty of the river
Will make you shiver,
Or maybe just grin with glee.

The river at rush
Is not a hush
But a soft and gentle gush.

Elliot Mills (9)
St Nicholas CE Primary School, Shepperton

Happy - Haikus

Monsters, aliens
Creeping out under our beds
Hope they don't get you!

Eyes are watching us
Peeping out ready to say
'*Boo!* I scare you too!'

Ready to scare us
Waking us up from our sleep
Be careful out there!

Angel Lily Grimmett (10)
St Nicholas CE Primary School, Shepperton

Storms

Crashing thunder
Wispy wind
Flashing lightning
Whizzing hurricanes
Choppy seas
Winter's breeze
Earthquakes shuddering
Tsunamis flooding.

Charlie Smith (9)
St Nicholas CE Primary School, Shepperton

Swimming

S wimming is so much fun
W hen you win a contest
 I n the sun
M y body loves to swim
M y body is fit to win
 I n the swimming pool I swim lots
N ever ever to stop
G reat is swimming.

Elisa Prater (9)
St Nicholas CE Primary School, Shepperton

Snow

I am cold
I am white
Sometimes very bright
I am here at Christmas
You are lucky if you see me
I come in January, February, November and December
What am I?
I am snow.

Holly Fraser (9)
St Nicholas CE Primary School, Shepperton

The Mermaid

As I dived into the clean blue water, I got a glimpse of one of the mermaids,
She was graceful as the pink glossy scarf around her gleaming, green scales,
The mermaid cupped her long, fine hand for me to land on,
She swished her yellowy-green tail this way and that,
In her hair lay a whale tooth comb with a pearl for a handle,
She was one of the most beautiful mermaids I had ever seen.

Jemima Worley-Smith (9)
St Nicholas CE Primary School, Shepperton

Ice Buns

I n the middle of the afternoon
C an we have one very soon?
E nough room to have one more

B eautiful icing I'm very sure
U nder my coat is where I hide it
N ever ever dislike it
S oon it is dessert ice buns.

Caris Oldman (9)
St Nicholas CE Primary School, Shepperton

Life

Life is an experience that we can all share,
Sometimes life can be very unfair,
Life can be amazing, fun or boring,
Especially when we're in bed snoring!

Susie Powell (10)
St Nicholas CE Primary School, Shepperton

Friendship

P eople come together after time and make friends, but nothing will take
  friends apart
O ften people soften, when children are open with friendship
E mbracing friendship with love equals happiness
M any people think that any type of person can make friendship
S ome people remain best friends forever.

Christina Castro-Wilkins (9)
St Nicholas CE Primary School, Shepperton

The Sky

Underneath the deep blue sky,
The little old elf can't believe his eyes,
He looked and he stared at the shimmering stars
And when he looked again, he could see Mars,
He said to himself, he will see the planets and the Milky Way,
One dark, glittering, shimmering night or day.

Freya Dight (9)
St Nicholas CE Primary School, Shepperton

Spain

S unny Spain, have a
P erfect holiday
A mazing places to have fun
I n the pool and on the beach
N ever go home!

Tom Corrigan (9)
St Nicholas CE Primary School, Shepperton

Lightning

Crash!
Bang! Flash!
The lightning thunders
Roaring with spite and
Full of anger and hate!

Katie Lawrence (9)
St Nicholas CE Primary School, Shepperton

Space

S pectacular solar system
P lanets all around
A liens, aliens, are they out there?
C louds hovering below
E verywhere, everywhere, planets are everywhere.

Harry Green (10)
St Nicholas CE Primary School, Shepperton

Food

F ood is amazing
O bviously it's all around the world
O f course, not everyone is fed in the world
D on't waste food.

Nicholas Murphy (9)
St Nicholas CE Primary School, Shepperton

Alligator Snapping Turtle
(Inspired by 'The Tyger' by William Blake)

Turtle, turtle, snapping fish
In the darkness of your wish.
What immortal jaws or stealth
Could frame thy fearful symmetry?

In what distant lake or river
Burnt the power of thine giver?
On what death dare he aspire?
What the shell dare seize the fire?

And what courage and what strength
Could twist the sinews of the heart?
And when thy jaw began to snap,
What dread fish? And what dread trap?

Turtle, turtle, snapping fish
In the darkness of your wish.
What immortal jaws or stealth
Could frame thy fearful symmetry?

Michael Aris Stam (8)
Sandford Primary School, Winscombe

147

The Komodo Dragon

(Inspired by 'The Tyger' by William Blake)

Komodo, komodo, chewing meat
In the darkness of the eat.
What immortal teeth or claws,
Could frame thy fearful symmetry?

In what distant rocks or shores
Whipped the tiger of thine jaws?
On what muscles dare crave?
What the claws dare seize the brave?

And what claws and what pest
Could twist the ribs of the breast?
And when thy lizard began to wake,
What legs did God make?

Komodo, komodo, chewing meat
In the darkness of the eat.
What immortal teeth or claws,
Dare frame thy fearful symmetry?

Joshua Green (9)
Sandford Primary School, Winscombe

The Dragon
(Inspired by 'The Tyger' by William Blake)

Dragon, dragon, breathing light,
In the darkness of the night.
What immortal wings or tail,
Could frame thy fearful symmetry?

In the distant skies or caves,
Burnt the humans with their braves?
On what prey dare he tire?
What the claw dare seize the fire?

And what wing and what scale,
Could twist the bone of the tail?
And when thy claw began to scrape
What dread fang? And what dread hate?

Dragon, dragon, breathing light
In the darkness of the night.
What immortal wings or tail,
Dare frame thy fearful symmetry?

Abigail Tucker (9)
Sandford Primary School, Winscombe

Sea Serpent

(Inspired by 'The Tyger' by William Blake)

Serpent, serpent, swimming low
In the lighting of the undertow.
What immortal tongue or tail,
Could frame thy whipping skinny tail?

In what distant underwater cave
Burn the scales of the brave?
On what teeth dare he desire?
What the fire dare seize the liar?

And what courage and what fear
Untwist the madness of thy heart?
And when thy tail began to whip,
What dread teeth and what dread flips?

Serpent, serpent, swimming low
In the lighting of the undertow.
What immortal tongue or tail,
Could frame thy whipping skinny tail?

Shoji Leach (9)
Sandford Primary School, Winscombe

Night

She's a dream of mine,
She has dazzling hair,
Her clothes are made of silk,
Her face is as pretty as a flower,
Her eyes are soft clouds,
She moves swiftly through the air,
She is called Melanie.

Tilly Penn (10)
Sibertswold CE Primary School, Shepherdswell

The Rustling Place

In the rustling place,
Children come to sit,
Amused by the wind chimes,
Rustling in the wind.

In the rustling place,
Frogs come to wade,
Tempted by the clear blue water,
Rippling in the wind.

In the rustling place,
Birds come to nest,
For they stumble across the waving trees,
Shaking in the wind.

In the rustling place,
Things rustled,
Things rippled,
Things shook,
In the rustling place.

Freya Wiltshire (10)
Sibertswold CE Primary School, Shepherdswell

Golden Sun

I see a sun, a golden sun,
It's not like any other sun,
It shines on me and it shines on you.

I am eating a golden bun,
In the sun
And then I see a waterfall.

I go to the waterfall,
I see the sun dripping gold into the waterfall,
Suddenly, the waterfall goes gold.

The sun is like a big, bouncy ball
Ready to bounce on you and me.

Abigail Oliver-Chastney (10)
Sibertswold CE Primary School, Shepherdswell

Night

Night is a girl,
She makes me feel loved,
Her face looks like the sun,
Her eyes are twinkling like stars,
Her mouth is as wide as the Pacific Ocean,
Her clothes are made of silk,
When she moves, she tiptoes,
When she talks, it is Canadian,
She lives in a cottage with her husband and a dog,
Night loves me,
Night is comforting,
Night makes me think of sweet dreams.

Sarah Chaplin (10)
Sibertswold CE Primary School, Shepherdswell

Night

In the night, lay a moon,
Whose peace is a delicate pearl.

Peace is her heart, her eyes, her mouth,
Her hair and her clothes.

Her heart is as red as a rose
And her eyes are as clear as a diamond.

Her clothes are soft, like silk,
Her mouth is a pink marshmallow and her teeth are stars.

When night comes, she tiptoes over to us
And gently spreads her light, which surrounds us with her safe glow.

Esmay Green (10)
Sibertswold CE Primary School, Shepherdswell

Night

Night is the Grim Reaper
He makes me feel cold
His face looks like a skull
His eyes are decomposed
His mouth is maggots eating his brain
His hair has worms crawling around it
His clothes are made of shadows
When he moves, darkness descends
When he speaks, death calls upon people
He lives in the Underworld, with the Devil and the Cyclops
Night haunts me.

Blake Roe (10)
Sibertswold CE Primary School, Shepherdswell

Night Cat

Creeping, sneaking, fast as light,
Sleek and shiny, blacker than night.
Emerald eyes, ebony waving tail,
Flexible, strong and yet quite frail.
Fast and beautiful in every way,
Running, spying, pouncing to catch its prey.
The sun rises, to home it will come,
So no one will know the crime it's done.

Aoife Baines (10)
Sibertswold CE Primary School, Shepherdswell

Gold

The gold rays glisten like golden sparkles,
In the middle of a field of golden sunflowers,
When night-time comes, no gold is near,
Only silver is here,
Morning comes with a golden glow,
Puddles of gold appear out of the rays,
Therefore everyone praises the gold.

Megan Wilshaw (10)
Sibertswold CE Primary School, Shepherdswell

Night

Night is a time to be scared.
He makes me feel like I'm lonely
And have nowhere to go!
His face is as dark as the night sky.
His eyes are like two piercing knives.
His mouth is as extensive as the moon.

Natasha Byrne (10)
Sibertswold CE Primary School, Shepherdswell

The Dreadful War

Eyes closed, heart pounding, bombs exploding,
My dad snoring like a piglet,
Eyes closed, heart pounding, bombs exploding,
I feel cold, damp and I have a lumpy pillow,
Eyes closed, heart pounding, bombs exploding,
I hear sirens ringing in my ears,
Eyes closed, heart pounding, bombs exploding,
Lancaster bombers so loud when they pass over,
Eyes closed, heart pounding, bombs exploding,
Drip, drip, drip, the water is dripping like a tap,
Eyes closed, heart pounding, bombs exploding,
My mum dropping off to sleep, like a baby falling to sleep,
Eyes closed, heart pounding, bombs exploding,
My friends are screaming, I hope they're OK!
Eyes closed, heart pounding, bombs exploding,
Clatter, clatter, clatter, bang, bang, bang!
Aeroplanes zooming over.

Jada Millward (9)
Thirsk CP School, Thirsk

War Is Here!

War is here,
I can hear the Spitfires.
War is here,
Bombs are dropping.
War is here,
We're stuffed in this tiny shelter.
War is here,
Firing of guns deafens me.
War is here,
Scared children wear their gas masks.
War is here,
When will it end, the guns and bombs?
War is here,
We want it to stop.
War is here,
We want just peace.
War is here,
We're closing in on them.
War is here,
It's ending today.
War is here,
It's peace in the world,
War is here,
Peace is here!

Emma Garthwaite (10)
Thirsk CP School, Thirsk

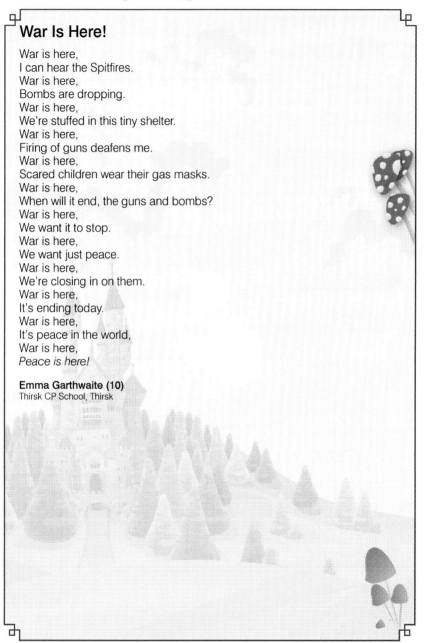

The Blitz

Boom! Boom! Bang! Bang!
Clatter! Clatter! Argh! Argh!
Boom! Boom! Bang! Bang!
Can't sleep, can't sleep,
Wonder if my house has fallen down?

Boom! Boom! Bang! Bang!
Clatter! Clatter! Argh! Argh!
Boom! Boom! Bang! Bang!
Can't sleep, can't sleep,
Wonder if my house has fallen down?

Boom! Boom! Bang! Bang!
Clatter! Clatter! Argh! Argh!

Darren Peckitt (10)
Thirsk CP School, Thirsk

The Shelter

The shelter was cruel,
I was cold,
So were the young,
So were the old.
I could hear the planes closing in,
I was wondering which Germans they would bring,
Houses were bursting into flames,
It was horrible, nasty,
Hitler was to blame.
The shelter was cruel,
I was cold,
So were the young,
So were the old.
It was horrible,
Cruel,
It was like drowning in a pool,
The shelter was cruel,
I was cold,
So were the young,
So were the old.

Amy Dickinson (9)
Thirsk CP School, Thirsk

Mistake

I tried to kill Hitler,
Which was probably a mistake,
For he had with him a sniper rifle
And a belt of steak,
He had with him a trench of Britons
And a 1930's car,
He had with him a super horse
And a delicious chocolate bar,
He had with him a Messerschmitt
And a gas mask,
He had with him a pile of bombs
And a big German task,
He had with him a damp pillow
And a bucket of mash,
But he missed out something important,
He forgot his tash!

Harry Collinson (10)
Thirsk CP School, Thirsk

War Shelters

Eyes closed, heart banging, bombs dropping
The shelter's leaking like a magical waterfall
Eyes closed, heart banging, bombs dropping
My father snoring like a bomb exploding
Eyes closed, heart banging, bombs dropping
My mother wide awake like an alert wolf
Eyes closed, heart banging, bombs dropping
My brother crying like an air raid siren going off
Eyes closed, heart banging, bombs dropping
Fires burning outside the shelters
Eyes closed, heart banging, bombs dropping
Planes crashing in the nearby streets
Eyes closed, heart banging, bombs dropping
I'm finally asleep.

Jordan Peacock (10)
Thirsk CP School, Thirsk

What War Feels Like

Eyes bloodshot, heart racing, bombs dropping,
Siren roaring like a lion,
Eyes bloodshot, heart racing, bombs dropping,
Spitfires zoom overhead,
Eyes bloodshot, heart racing, bombs dropping,
Dog snoring like Grandad,
Eyes bloodshot, heart racing, bombs dropping,
House suddenly in flames,
Eyes bloodshot, heart racing, bombs dropping,
Then . . . no house!
Eyes bloodshot, heart racing, bombs dropping,
'When will it end?'

Allan Hudson (10)
Thirsk CP School, Thirsk

Blitz

Boom! Boom! Boom! Bombs drop from every angle
Lamp posts are blacked out with luminous paper
I stumble as the bomb detonator goes off in front of me
They break the silence as they bomb us
Zooming planes fly over the British army.

Ben Calvert (10)
Thirsk CP School, Thirsk

World At War

War! War! When does it end?
Bombs booming in my ears.
Sounds of men and women shouting in my ear, 'Run! Run!'
I hear my mum shouting for me to come back,
I run and run to the shelter,
A bomb drops right in front of me.
I try to run away from it, but it is too late,
The bomb loses its last spark,
Then *boom!* The bomb explodes,
It pushes me down,
I manage to stay alive!

Abby Faulkner (9)
Thirsk CP School, Thirsk

Boom! Boom! Crash!

The war is a black ghost,
The smoky smell of dropping bombs,
The rattle of the Spitfire,
My heart is racing,
I have goosebumps on my cheeks,
We run into our shelters,
Boom! Boom! Crash! go the bombs,
The baby is squealing,
The shelters are dark,
Boom! Boom! Crash! go the bombs!

Will Gascoigne (9)
Thirsk CP School, Thirsk

The Exploding War

War is a big, black, angry cloud
The ear-piercing sound of the air raid siren wailing and screaming
Then *bang!*
I'm scared, I don't know what to do
Should I hide?
I see German planes entering, more and more pouring in
Argh! Bombs! I should run,
Bang! Bang! Bang! There are people running wildly,
Screaming and shouting, dogs barking,
This war will never end, will it?

Holly Elliott (10)
Thirsk CP School, Thirsk

All I Can Hear Is The Blitz

Boom! Boom! Bang! Bang!
All I hear is the dropping of bombs blowing up my house
The air raid siren, my heart beating
Shouting for my mum, she is laying dead
My eyes water, I take her to shelter with my family
The all-clear siren does not go for what seems like a year
Then it happens; the all-clear siren goes!
Victory! We can go back inside my house
It is destroyed! What will I do now?

Ben Laws-Williams (10)
Thirsk CP School, Thirsk

Soldier

As he runs through no-man's-land,
With his gun,
His heart thumping,
His teeth chattering,
His ears picking up the sounds of bombs and bullets,
His nose smelling the smoke from blazing fires,
Burning buildings and much, much more,
But . . . he still runs,
Bullets and bombs avoiding this brave World War II soldier!

Millie Ann Cuthbert (10)
Thirsk CP School, Thirsk

The Anderson Shelter

Eyes closed, thumping chest, damp pillow
Grandad snoring like a Lancaster bomber
Eyes closed, thumping chest, damp pillow
Brother crying like an air raid siren
Eyes closed, thumping chest, damp pillow
Sister sewing silently like still water
Eyes closed, thumping chest, damp pillow
Mother snoring like a sleeping cat.

Harry Lamb (10)
Thirsk CP School, Thirsk

The War

Eyes closed, heart pounding, wind blowing
Siren wailing, like a hurricane
Eyes closed, heart pounding, wind blowing
Father snoring, like a windy day
Eyes closed, wind blowing, heart pounding
Bombers flying over, swooping in the air
People hoping that their homes are still there
Eyes closed, wind blowing, heart pounding.

Charlie Pritchard (10)
Thirsk CP School, Thirsk

Tragedy Everywhere

B *oom! Boom!* go the bombs as they hit the floor
L oads of people dying every second
A t any time the air raid sirens go off
C locks tick hoping the war will end
K ids and adults very scared
O range flames spitting everywhere
U ncontrollable fires are very hard to put out
T ragic things happen in war.

Billy Corser (10)
Thirsk CP School, Thirsk

The Anderson Shelter

My body is shaking, bombs are dropping
Planes are roaring, people screaming
Like air raid sirens
My body is shaking, bombs are dropping
Planes are roaring, mother is snoring
Loudly like an elephant charging
My body is shaking, bombs are dropping
Planes are roaring.

Sam Hudson (10)
Thirsk CP School, Thirsk

The Destiny Pilots

A eroplanes are being shot down
I mpact as it hits the ground
R etreat into the tubes

R oaring bombs over our heads
A eroplanes are shooting over our heads
I magine what's happening up there
D estiny is going to be ours.

Lewis Sage (9)
Thirsk CP School, Thirsk

The Anderson Shelter

Eyes closed, heart beating, bombs dropping
Mother sleeping like a baby
Eyes closed, heart beating, bombs dropping
Brother is reading his big book quietly
Eyes closed, heart beating, bombs dropping
Sister writing out her hard homework
Eyes closed, heart beating, bombs dropping.

Shannon Moore (9)
Thirsk CP School, Thirsk

The Lady Riding

She rides astride,
The mighty beast,
Of this jungle.

She flames with fury,
A child not stolen,
She fears.

The great beast growls,
Then with her fears forgotten,
She looks up.

Her eyes are as red,
As the planet above us,
She smiles.

I stumble back,
In my dark, green hideout,
I'm gone.

Lucie Rowland (10)
Vaughan Primary School, West Harrow

The Day The Martians Came

The day the Martians came,
A day not to be remembered,
It all started upon,
The 18th of September;

The day the Martians came,
Caused a lot of havoc
And in the rain they sleep,
In scruffy little hammocks!

The day the Martians came,
Gave us all a nasty fright,
They attacked Buckingham Palace,
They were spoiling for a fight;

The day the Martians came,
They were cheating in a game,
They're really, really gross,
They lay eggs in human brains!

The day the Martians came,
Started off rather fine,
Then they found a forest,
Now they live in Bristlecone Pines;

The day the Martians came,
Was very, very scary,
Their names are very weird,
Their leader was called Airy!

The day the Martians came,
A day not to be remembered,
It all started upon,
The 18th of September.

Matthew Barnes-Murphy (10)
Vaughan Primary School, West Harrow

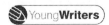

Run

I'm playing happily with the others,
Then suddenly, I hear my mother.

She's calling me,
I hear her shout, 'Run!'

She trumpets and trumpets, but suddenly there's silence,
I turn around; 'How could anyone do this?'

I run, I run and run, until I can run no more,
I turn around, aliens I saw.

They were running too, after me,
But they had something of my mother's, so I ran - towards them.

I was angrier than I've ever been,
The angriest elephant you've ever seen.

I charged and charged and butted its stomach,
I'm only a baby, with no luck;

To help me survive on my own,
What am I going to do?

But the alien solved that problem
By saying, 'I'm going to kill you!'

Eliana Lovell (11)
Vaughan Primary School, West Harrow

Winter

I'm the coldest of the seasons,
I covered the world in a white blanket,
Children wake up and run outside,
Snowball fights and snowmen games are played,
After a great play in the snow,
Children run inside,
Where hot chocolate and a fire greets them,
When they go in, more children come out,
I always have children to play with,
But I don't last forever,
Make the most of me before I go,
I hope you love the snow!

Jake Walker-Charles (10)
Vaughan Primary School, West Harrow

The Dragon

The dragon's eye sees all,
Staring, glaring,
The world beneath the dragon's feet,
The dragon's mouth devours,
Chewing, swallowing,
Fire blazing from the dragon's mouth,
The dragon's claws destroys,
Ripping, shredding,
Demolishing without mercy,
The dragon's wing slaps through the air,
Swooshing, speeding,
Causing hurricanes,
The dragon's scales shields even bullets,
As dark as night, as black as pitch,
Is there no end to this colossal animal?

Joe Molander (11)
Vaughan Primary School, West Harrow

Mansion

Once I was in a mansion,
A very scary mansion,
Where ghosts and ghouls pick their noses,
Here and there and everywhere!
Where vampires drink the cheapest of blood,
They leave the tap on and create a flood,
Zombies coming from Bombay,
To have a marvellous day,
OK, OK, it's not so scary,
Anyway, it's time to play!

Gabrielle Gez (10)
Vaughan Primary School, West Harrow

The Octopus

The octopus is the DJ of the sea,
Everyone loves his rap,
He's very cool, unlike school,
He'll make you cheer and clap.

He wears his shades around the ocean,
Dancing on the ocean floor,
People cheer, they shout there and here
And they just want a whole lot more.

The octopus is green with spots,
He has green stripes on his face,
He wears Lycra shorts when he's doing sports,
Especially in a race!

He sings a song walking down the street,
Singing, *'La, di, doo, da, dee!'*
He sings the song, walking up and along,
The octopus is definitely the coolest in the sea!

Imogen Pursglove (10)
Vaughan Primary School, West Harrow

Sky

The sky is high,
In June, July,
The sky is blue,
In winter too!
Clouds fill the sky,
From top to toe,
The birds fly,
Sun or snow!
Every night planes fly by,
Just look up, they're really high,
Shining sun in the sky,
Glistening moon waving bye!
Stars sparkle, stars glow,
They look like little drops of snow,
Even if there's lots to do,
Sky stands out for me and you!

Agni Amani Choudhury (11)
Vaughan Primary School, West Harrow

Death Awaits You

I lay on my bed and stare at the ceiling,
Why do I have to be a human being?
My heart is shattered,
No one else mattered,
I hate being a human being!

I have dark circles around my eyes,
Forever my heart dies,
My eyes are sore and puffy,
I cannot gulp my coffee,
My heart still painfully dies.

The floor moves and blurs below me,
I cannot forget what she did for me,
It feels like I cannot live anymore,
My body feels sore,
I cannot ever forget what she did for me.

Why did the dreaded BMW kill her?
Take her?
Send her?
Jilly, oh Jilly, come back to me,
Don't you see?
I miss her.

Now I am a sad, useless rag,
I remember playing tag,
It hurts to think about it,
My heart is broken to little bits.

She's gone . . .
Forever!

Aathirai Lingarajah (10)
Vaughan Primary School, West Harrow

Fluttering Fairies And Blue-Eyed Goblins

I've stepped into this wonderland,
Everything around me is magical,
Fluttering fairies and blue-eyed goblins.

I step under a tree and a cloud of fairy dust comes down on me
Surrounding me with magical powers.
Everywhere I dance, I feel as if I'm flying, just like the fluttering fairies.
Every time I laugh, I feel as if I'm giggling with the goblins and their jokes.

I've stepped into this wonderland,
Everything around me is magical,
Fluttering fairies and blue-eyed goblins.

I go to the palace and the fairy king greets me
With my own pair of fairy wings wrapped in gold silk lace.
Everywhere I go I jump for joy at the magical views.
Every time I whisper a fluttering fairy whispers back.

I've stepped out of this wonderland,
Everything around me has gone,
No fluttering fairies or blue-eyed goblins,
I'm here, back in my bed.

Millie Chisholm (10)
Vaughan Primary School, West Harrow

A Minx

A minx is cheeky and mischievous,
Skipping lightly on her feet.
Thinking she's pretty and glorious,
Oh, what a little cheat!

She runs around all day,
But never does she know,
What to say,
When her mother asks, 'Blow, have you been all day?'

She's never hot,
She's never cold,
She sits in a cot
And she's told about her amazing plot.

Elani Jeyagugan (10)
Vaughan Primary School, West Harrow

My Sister's Really Massive Temper

Everyone thinks my sister's sweet and cute,
But really she's a monster with a really massive temper,
Outside she's girlie and mute,
She hypnotises my family, what a mischievous little brute!

My sister is not very human at all,
I wish the Doctor would come in his TARDIS
And save the world from my sister, I call,
D'you know once she was so bad and wrecked the Sheffield mall?

My sister's so angry now, she could build a twister,
'Oh no! Oh no!' I scream and shout,
But that's not cos of my blister,
I'm shouting that because of my terrible, terrible sister!

Dhani Ratna (10)
Vaughan Primary School, West Harrow

Her Face

Her face, her face was as pretty as a princess,
Her hair, her hair was as golden as the sun,
Her eyes began to shine when she opened the window,
The robins began to tweet when she sang.

Her voice was as lovely as an opera singer,
Her teeth were as white as her mum's,
Her eyelashes were the longest you had ever seen,
The robins began to tweet as she sang.

Shannen McPhail (10)
Vaughan Primary School, West Harrow

169

The Shadow

The shadow is dark,
Reflected on tree bark.

The shadow is cold,
But also big and bold.

The shadow is eerie,
But kind? Not nearly!

The shadow is a monster!
So never ever cross her!

The shadow is a meanie,
But definitely not teeny!

So cross her never ever
If you want to live forever!

Alice Agerbak (10)
Vaughan Primary School, West Harrow

My Imagination

My imagination is like a hippy van full of dangerous guns
Lockers full of fat leprechauns
Haunted schools full of werewolves
Big boats in the sea full of ghosts
Scary planets full of flesh-eating aliens
The cargo ship's full of food and terrifying cousins.

Luke Parmar (10)
Victoria Primary School, Carrickfergus

School

    S   ensational
    C   leverness
    H   appiness
c O   -operation
    O   utside playing
    L   earning.

Sarah Louise Hoyles (10)
Warren Hills CP School, Coalville

The Moon

The moon is a big lump of cheese
Rotating round the Earth
It is a bouncy ball bouncing round the sky
The moon is a bright light shimmering out of nowhere
It is a white blob of paint
Painted on a thick black sheet
The moon is a round biscuit, hard and very scrumptious.

Lauren Douglas (10)
Ysgol Hiraddug, Dyserth

Young Writers Information

We hope you have enjoyed reading this
book - and that you will continue to enjoy it
in the coming years.

If you like reading and writing poetry drop
us a line, or give us a call, and we'll send
you a free information pack.

Alternatively, if you would like to order further
copies of this book or any of our other titles,
then please give us a call or log onto our
website at www.youngwriters.co.uk.

Young Writers Information
Remus House
Coltsfoot Drive
Peterborough
PE2 9BF
Tel: (01733) 890066
Fax: (01733) 313524

Email: info@youngwriters.co.uk